PMDD:
A Handbook for Partners

PMDD:
A Handbook for Partners

Living on a Prayer
Living with PMDD

Liana Laverentz

PMDD: A Handbook for Partners

Lily Pond Publications

Cover Art by *Rae Monet, Inc. Design*

Living on a Prayer, Living with PMDD
P.O. Box 196
Harborcreek, PA 16421-0196
www.livingwithpmdd.com

Publishing History
First Edition, December, 2015
Print ISBN 978-1-943734-03-0
Digital ISBN 978-1-943734-02-3

Published in the United States of America

Disclaimer

This book's intention is to inform and educate. It is not to replace medical advice provided by your partner's health care professional, be that a physician, physician's assistant, or nurse practitioner. It is recommended that your partner consult her doctor or health professional before following any therapeutic suggestions offered here, especially if she has any pre-existing medical condition(s), but especially any involving her endocrine or autoimmune system. She should never reduce or discontinue her prescribed medication(s) without the consent of her doctor. The author cannot take medical or legal responsibility for illness arising out of failure to seek medical advice from a medical professional, or failure to take medications as prescribed.

Also, per the Terms of Agreement regarding content on my Living on a Prayer, Living with PMDD blog, all reader comments are presented as anonymous and used with permission.

Praise for Living on a Prayer, Living with PMDD

———◆———

Your writing gives both hope and comfort, not to mention the advice is truly good and might save someone from this suffering.

୬ᐟୢ

Great help...I needed this so bad because as a man I never understood this because I don't have it but reading this may have just saved my relationship... Thanks.

୬ᐟୢ

My wife and I have been together for 17 years and I've only just discovered your blog. For 17 years I've wondered exactly what has been wrong, and now I finally know.

୬ᐟୢ

Thank you so much for this. It so totally spoke to and of me, I could hardly finish the article for the tears in my eyes. Someone understands what I'm living with.

୬ᐟୢ

My husband said it's like someone has been living in our house and recording everything we go through.

୬ᐟୢ

Thank you so much for giving me hope, 30 years of the same kind of PMDD as you describe. Am also drug free for ten years after being used as a human guinea pig by so-called professionals. Being told there is no such thing as PMDD, at the same time giving me coils that release hormones, hormone replacement therapy and SSRI's at the same time.

୬ᐟୢ

I have no close friends; most people think I am crazy and when I try to explain to them I sound even crazier. So I live in isolation mostly and have to pretend I am okay when I see people. My mother has tried to have me admitted a few times. Only my son and daughter get the real me and my PMDD and if it was not for them I am sure I would have taken my own life by now. Thank you so much, you make me feel like holding on and living.

⁓ᴗ⁓

This is SUCH good advice! Thank you for continuing to give encouragement and suggestions for how to help, other than pushing meds that do exactly what you said - create side effects to add onto the stress one is already dealing with!

⁓ᴗ⁓

I want to thank you for bringing rationality to something that is so inherently irrational. For the past two years, I've been coping with the realization that my life-long "insanity" is PMDD. All this time, I've been single. Now, I've met someone new and have not yet told him the "evil truth." Your blog is fantastic and really helps me to understand how to approach my new situation with this someone special. Thank you.

Excerpts from PMDD:
A Handbook for Partners

———◆———

The worst part of it is the uncertainty. I know that at some point my wife is going to change and project a thousand negative emotions right into my head, then be as calm and as normal and loving as the girl I fell in love with, but with no acknowledgment of the turmoil that just ripped straight through the heart of our relationship.

⁓⁓

I'm happy to have this info, because at least I can see I'm not alone and as hard as it is to believe during an episode, it's not her fault. It's so hard not to take it personal when she is so cold and vicious.

⁓⁓

I think I have PMDD. I just realized that every month for a couple of days I feel very irritable, I even rage and normally I am a very calm person. I feel like quitting my job and I question every single aspect of my life. Last week I put my relationship at risk because I behaved very badly with my bf. I embarrassed him in front of his friends and on our way home I screamed, I hit him, and I told him he could walk away from me.

⁓⁓

We have been in an episode for 15 days now, this is the longest lasting one. Probably because her period is over a week late. it feels like i am fighting for my life, and the pure hatred towards me is harsh. When she gets her period this all goes away and we have a week of normal till it starts again.

⁓⁓

I have been in and out of a relationship with the same wonderful woman for three years. She has broken up with me anywhere from 7-9 times. It is absolutely predictable. The break ups are inexplicable and all happen right before her period. During or after her period she loves me again and wants to get back together with me...anywhere from two to five days after we break up we are back together.

⁓ꞋⱾ⸱⁓

I may also suffer from anxiety separate from PMDD and sometimes I cannot escape those terrifying feelings of no control ... I'm so afraid of those who think its PMS because my only defense is, "No, it's different, far more intense." "Yeah, that's what each woman says about their period." "No, really, I consider suicide once a month like clockwork, and that's not normal." "Oh, more drama..." These are conversations I've had and fear I'll have again.

⁓ꞋⱾ⸱⁓

The first step is making the choice to figure it out for the both of you. Then figuring her out, and then you have to figure yourself out, and stop yourself from reacting. Once you've managed all that then you need to try and talk to her, help her help herself. This is hard because as far as she knows, it's you that has the problem.

Dedication

To partners of women with PMDD everywhere

Table of Contents

Author's Note

PMDD: A Handbook for Partners is a spinoff of my book *PMDD and Relationships*, which is based in part on several blog posts I wrote between May 2010 and May 2015. In each of these two books I have updated the affected blog posts to reflect the most current information available at publication. If you click on the link that leads you to the blog post, you may find differences between the posts and these chapters. That only means I have not yet updated all of the original blog posts to reflect the latest information.

Other sections of this book are new material, and information provided in them may be repeated in other titles in my PMDD series, the availability of which can be found on my blog or website.

This book is not intended to be read like a novel, rather more like a reference book. If you do read it all the way through, some information may be repeated. If you are only looking for information on what to do during an acute episode of PMDD, skip directly to Chapter Thirteen. The rest of the book, however, will provide information on insight into your partner with PMDD's thought processes during an episode of PMDD, what contributes to PMDD, and how to improve your relationship over time.

November 2015

A few years ago I read a book by a famous television personality on happiness, or how to be happy. By all accounts, according to that book, I should have been the happiest woman on the planet. In case I might be missing a few opportunities for happiness, it offered seventeen powerful tips for living a happier life. All of which I at the time already practiced regularly, if not daily.

But still, then and now, on some days happiness eludes me. Why is this? Because there are times you simply cannot be happy when you have PMDD, also known as the mood disorder Pre-Menstrual Dysphoric Disorder.

Plain and simple, during an episode of PMDD, nothing makes you happy. No-thing. You can have fleeting moments of pleasure, but that's all they are. Fleeting.

Let's break it down. PMDD. That first D stands for Dysphoric, the opposite of euphoric. Euphoric means happy, dysphoric means depressed. As in depression. The kind of depression suffered by at least the 164 million people in the United States who were given prescriptions for antidepressants in 2008 alone. No one knows how many more there are, not being treated with drug therapy, talk therapy, or any other kind of therapy. Depression, while not a rich man's disease, can only be diagnosed and treated if you have the means and mindset to see a doctor and pay for the treatment.

But PMDD is different. PMDD is a disorder that comes and goes in concert with a woman's menstrual cycle. Actually, disorder is misleading. PMDD is more than a simple disorder of the mind, as defined by the DSM-5 (the bible of the American Psychiatric Association). If left untreated, PMDD can expand in scope from 2-3 days a month to *all but* 2-3 days a month, or until a woman is left with no "good days" to enjoy.

PMDD can be inherited, and can begin as early as a woman's first period. Mostly, according to medical experts on the subject, the onset arrives in a woman's twenties or thirties, and if left untreated, grows progressively worse until menopause.

As I look back on my life, I can see I was an early starter. I remember an episode in college that kept me in bed for three weeks, feeling listless, hopeless, and lethargic. Then suddenly it disappeared, and I had to work like a maniac to complete all my coursework and pass the semester.

I've often likened my life to that of a salmon swimming upstream. Always behind, always swimming against the tide, never managing to fully get where I am going. For years I thought it was my time-management skills. Now I realize it was the PMDD kicking my butt.

When I'm not in the throes of PMDD, I can get more done in a day than four people and get more done in a week than most people can in a month. I've managed projects, contests, social events, PR events, organized banquets, grand openings, conferences, committees, written five books, edited over seventy-five more, and designed and overseen the building of two houses. I've won awards for most of those things, and have the certificates, plaques, clocks, and trophies to show for it.

When I'm having a PMDD episode, I can barely shower and get dressed. My mind is fuzzy and disoriented, my thoughts scattered, my emotions raw and unstable. I ache all over physically, my brain either feels like it's burning or has an iron band wrapped around it, I feel like I am moving through molasses, and I have absolutely no motivation. I don't want to see anybody, much less talk to them, or do much of anything. My prevailing thought patterns are, "Why bother? Nobody cares anyway. What's the use?" and "Take me now, Lord. Just get it over with and take me. I can't possibly be of use to anyone in this state."

Every negative thought is magnified until I am practically paralyzed as far as decision making goes. That includes decisions as simple as what to eat or wear. What if I screw up, make the wrong choice? I know I will—my PMDD brain is telling me it's inevitable. My PMDD brain is also telling me that to make such a mistake would be the end of the world.

And I believe it.

Like I said, undiagnosed PMDD can only get worse over time. It can also predispose you toward major depressive episodes, both in response to life stresses and during times when women are most vulnerable to depression, such as post-partum, and peri- and post-menopausal. In 2009 I had an episode that lasted for weeks and weeks and weeks, which set me on the path to starting my blog, Living on a Prayer, Living with PMDD.

I now know that back then I was experiencing a low-grade perimenopausal depression that my PMDD exacerbated until it became unbearable. It forced me to take the time out to see to my own health and wellness—to put *me* first.

Why didn't I do something about my PMDD earlier? Well, for the first 25 years, I didn't know PMDD existed. I just thought I had regular PMS, and since 80% of menstruating women experience some symptoms of PMS, I didn't see why I couldn't just deal with it like everyone else. Was I really that incapable of coping with something women deal with every day? My pride refused to allow for that possibility.

Besides, the episodes came and went. And as soon as they went, I was too busy playing catch up to stop and try to figure out what was wrong with me. All I knew was I was free to be myself again, and frankly, for those first 25 years, out of sight was out of mind. I was just grateful to be back on track again.

Until the next time. For years, I consoled myself with the idea that "this too, shall pass," and in a few days it would be over. I could then get on with my life again, as a wife, mother, part-time office worker, and writer. I didn't realize what a huge disservice I was doing to myself, allowing my PMDD to progress. Besides, I still thought it was simple PMS, and all the prevailing medical literature at the time said there was nothing I could do but "live with it." To be sure, there were lifestyle and dietary changes I could make, and off and on I tried. But every effort seemed to fail after a few weeks, and I thought it was due to a lack of willpower.

Wrong. It was the PMDD. PMDD being cyclical as it is, what starts out as a brilliant idea and the willpower and determination behind it, all too soon devolves into a stupid idea with no willpower or motivation to support it. Sometimes this change in perception comes as soon as two weeks after the onset of your period, sometimes you're blessed with a full three weeks before your world view turns upside down again. Your PMDD brain is also a crafty character, and very adaptable to change—or, rather, finding ways to subvert any positive changes you may make.

PMDD is all about self-preservation, believe me. There's nothing your PMDD brain won't do to keep running the show. When women commit suicide to escape their PMDD, chances are they feel it's the only way to shut up the bully in their PMDD brain.

PMDD can strike both around the time of a woman's ovulation, *and* pre-menstrually. It can also occur post-menstrually in atypical cases—which was what confused me for so many years. It wasn't until 2010 that I learned it could also occur *after* your period begins. Mine comes without fail on the third day of my period—when it chooses to come. It doesn't come every month, and sometimes it comes twice a month, which only adds to the confusion. For years I had only mild symptoms pre-menstrually, mostly food cravings and anger, edginess and irritation, with my major depressive symptoms coming *after* my period started.

All the literature I read said the symptoms of PMDD came only pre-menstrually. So I didn't feel I could qualify for a diagnosis of PMDD. Something else had to be going on with me, in addition to what I thought was ordinary PMS, but it didn't have a name that I could find, and I didn't know how to go about explaining it to anyone.

To tell the truth, I just thought I was crazy.

In the past few years, however, my symptoms have come pre-menstrually, post-menstrually, and during what I call "special" months, during ovulation. I would barely get over one episode before another began, until early 2009, when I had one that lasted five weeks.

It was after the five-week episode that I knew I had to do something. I couldn't afford to lose weeks of productivity at a time. I knew I wasn't depressed, not in the way of Major Depressive Disorder, because the symptoms came and went. Finally I started charting them, and after two months, per the instructions in all the books I read, I went to my doctor and was diagnosed with PMDD.

That's when the real fun began. Now that my PMDD had been confirmed, it was time to read (and in many cases, re-read) everything I possibly could about it. I had been collecting information about PMS and PMDD for years. Since 1985. But I hadn't looked into it seriously since 1994, when I read *Women's Bodies, Women's Wisdom*, by Dr. Christiane Northrup.

Unfortunately, at the time, in all but a few medical research circles, PMDD was still a faraway blip on the general public's horizon. Most of the information available to the general public at that time was about PMS, with references to PMDD as simply a "more severe" form of PMS—which has since been proven through clinical studies to be untrue.

PMDD is a medical condition separate and apart from PMS. However, since it affects women, and occurs as part of our menstrual cycles, it's still lumped in with PMS and PME, or Pre-Menstrual Exacerbation, of existing disorders (such as arthritis, asthma, lupus, fibromyalgia, diabetes, and yes, depression).

I wasn't crazy. This really was happening. And there was a medical explanation for it. My body was not working properly during those times of the month. This malfunction made me edgy, angry, weepy, sad, muddle-headed and hungry. It was okay, though. All I had to do was watch my diet, take vitamins, exercise, maintain a healthy weight, listen to the wisdom of my body, rest when I could, and grin and bear it when I couldn't.

So I did—until, like I said, the episodes started lasting eight to ten days, and then weeks at a time. Until I discovered the latest research on PMDD, produced in the past decade, which states that no matter what you do, as long as your *brain* does not work properly, no amount of healthy eating, exercise, vitamins or herbs, meditation exercises, motivational books and CDs, self-talk, psychological counseling, or acts of goodwill will eliminate your PMDD.

All of the above will no doubt make your partner with PMDD healthier overall, and may make her feel better more days than not, but they will *not* make her PMDD go away.

Not by themselves, that is.

Knowledge is power, and with the information included in this book, you will have the basic tools needed to create a better relationship with your partner with PMDD, and to come to understand and deal with her PMDD at *your* speed and level.

Introduction

---◆---

Creating my Living With PMDD Blog

Living With PMDD Blog

Hi, I'm Liana, and for the past 40+ years I've had PMDD. The first 25 years I had no idea what was going on inside me, and I simply thought I was crazy. Not wanting anyone else to know that, I kept it to myself. For the next ten years, I knew something was wrong, but not that there was anything I could do about it. So I coped the best I could. Only in the past seven years have I discovered what PMDD really is and that there are as many ways to manage it as there are women who have it, which is reported at 3-8%, and sometimes up to 10%, of all menstruating women.

PMDD is not a one-size-fits-all disorder. Even the experts can't agree on what it is, what causes it, or how to treat it. So how are ordinary people like me, you, or your partner supposed to figure it out? But we are trying—in droves. It is for all of us with PMDD—and the partners who love us—that I have written my PMDD books.

Since I started researching this disorder in earnest seven years ago, I've discovered all sorts of information that is readily available, but not all in one place. The number of PMDD sites that have sprung up in the past two years alone, since PMDD was included as a full-blown mental disorder in the DSM-5, is overwhelming. But what I've noticed is each site has its own slant/angle/agenda, and no one site is a resource for all things PMDD, which would allow each woman to fully research her individual options.

So I decided to create a site with that goal in mind. To have one site that connects with other legitimate sites (as opposed to, say, advertisements disguised as websites) and would allow women the opportunity to figure out for ourselves what applies in our cases and what doesn't. I know what works for me. But I also know that what works for me may well not work for millions of other women—so telling you what works for me is a shot in the dark at best.

Still, there needs to be a reliable place where people can come to sort through their loved one's PMDD issues. Thus my blog Living on a Prayer, Living with PMDD was born. Why Living on a Prayer? Faith has been a vital part of my journey toward understanding myself and my PMDD. I wouldn't have been able to reach the level of wellness I have without it. That's not to say faith is the only thing that will get you through your partner's PMDD. Just that it helps enormously, and you might want to try it. But whether you believe in a Divine Power or not, you still need faith in something to help your partner manage her PMDD.

I say manage because despite what countless websites and medical professionals might tell you, ***there is no cure for PMDD***. The most your partner can hope to do is manage her symptoms, and maybe send those symptoms into remission for a while. But for her to do that successfully, you both need faith in something—faith in yourselves, and faith in your relationship.

My first step toward managing my PMDD was to get to know myself, to like myself, to trust myself, and to learn how to listen to myself—and not to anyone or anything outside my body. That's not to say I don't listen to the experts. I still read everything I can find on the subject. But I filter that information through my mind and heart and body based on my forty-plus years of experience with PMDD and what I now know about myself. I listen to my body when I try any new practice or treatment, and fine tune things as I go.

As of this writing I am not PMDD-free, but I am drug and surgery free and able to function every day of the month. Some days I have to take it easier than others, for sure, but I'm no longer incapacitated by my PMDD and I no longer suffer from all the fallout that PMDD causes in our lives such as broken relationships, unhealthy addictions, and the overwhelming negativity that sabotages our joy, creativity, and positive thoughts.

In my blog, I've shared my journey with PMDD. In this book, I want to provide some tools and resources you can use to help you to have a happier relationship with the woman you love.

I also want to make sure you know that while PMDD is not normal, your partner is still a normal woman with normal thoughts and emotions, needs, hopes, dreams, and fears. It is the PMDD that magnifies her normal thoughts and emotions, hopes, dreams, needs, and fears into something else, something totally overwhelming, and makes her overreact in irrational and extreme ways. But the root hopes and fears, worries and concerns, issues and emotions that she faces each and every day are the same as those of any other woman.

It is the PMDD that is abnormal. Not her. **She is not her PMDD.** She is not damaged or broken. Quite the opposite. She is stronger than either of you know.

My hope is that by the end of this book you will have come to accept that while PMDD is something you must deal with, and deal with together, *it does not have to define your relationship.*

And it most certainly does not have to control it.

Chapter One

———◆———

Relationships are Hard

Relationships are hard, no matter who you are, or what your situation is. Relationships for a woman with PMDD can be almost impossible to sustain, because, due to our hormonal fluctuations, we're literally a different woman every day. We feel differently, think differently, and act differently *every single day*.

There's an old joke that goes: A woman marries a man thinking he will change. A man marries a woman thinking she won't change.

Unfortunately, both end up being disappointed.

Change is inevitable. That's our only guarantee in life, short of death and taxes. Life comes and goes in cycles, and nothing stays the same. You will change, I will change, and your family and/or partner will change. Your circumstances, situations and environments will change, physically, mentally, emotionally, spiritually, financially, and otherwise. Accept that now, and you'll be a lot further ahead of the game than most of us.

Why? Because nobody likes change, even when it's for the better. Change takes work, motivation, and concentration, whether it's a change we embrace (like maybe a new move or a new job or a new baby), or a change we resist (like maybe a new move or a new job or a new baby). It all depends on your perspective.

But in general, women like to be comfortable in our surroundings and relationships. We like knowing what we're in for, how our day will go, what we're up against, what to expect. A certain stability gives us a good foundation for dealing with all the surprises life throws our way, be they blessings or challenges.

A woman with PMDD, just like anyone else, likes to have stability in her life. Unfortunately, that's not a luxury we can rely on, given the rocky ups and downs caused by our menstrual cycles. And what affects us, affects our friends, relatives, and partners. It takes an incredible amount of inner strength to be the kind of woman we want to be, especially when our brains won't work right. Even the most patient and loving person loses it at times. So how can you expect your partner to be any better, or different?

To those who have asked if it is even possible for a woman with PMDD to have a solid, steady, loving relationship, the short answer is yes. The longer answer is it will take work on both sides of the relationship.

The first step is awareness. Both you and your partner with PMDD will have to realize and accept that her PMDD is a living, breathing part of her, and isn't going to go away, not without both of you working together to make some serious changes in your life together. The more awareness you have, the better, and the better she will feel, but the PMDD never really goes away. You will have to stay vigilant—together as a team— because when she slips, as we all inevitably do, there's a very good chance her symptoms will return, and sometimes worse than before.

So how do the two of you gain this awareness? She, by taking the time to listen to her body and be good to herself. You, by being observant and possibly helping her to be pro- active. You can't *make* her do anything. But you can *help* her. Help her to understand that her first and most important relationship in this life (aside from her relationship with God, which is not the focus of this book) needs to be the relationship she has with...

Herself.

Not you.

Are you surprised? Disappointed? Confused?

The truth is your partner with PMDD needs to be able to give to/take care of herself, before she can truly take care of/give to anyone else. If you want to have any hope of having your relationship succeed in a healthy way...each of you has to put your own wellness needs first. I say this because many women are so conditioned to take care of others first, that we haven't the foggiest idea of how to put ourselves first without feeling enormously guilty, or without making those around us feel enormously guilty.

Nobody ends up happy when that happens.

Most women with PMDD spend a lot of time hating ourselves. Beating ourselves up, for things over which we have no control—in particular the way our PMDD negatively magnifies our thoughts and moods, which then affects our words and actions.

So the first thing she has to do, no matter how awful she may think she is, or might have been to you or others in the past, is to stop beating herself up. Neither of you can benefit from her dragging all that baggage from past PMDD episodes into today. Let go of it and start anew. Today is a new day, and today both of you are going to start being good to yourselves, if only for a few minutes.

Because change is hard, and works best if you tackle it in baby steps. Not many women can suddenly start shoving everyone else aside to carve out time to be good to themselves. We have commitments and responsibilities, and—if we're very lucky—people and partners who depend on us for some measure of support, comfort, and stability.

The bottom line is she needs to find something of her own that makes her happy, and find a way to do it. This is not being selfish. Nobody should deny her the time and space she needs to soothe her spirit and settle herself. It may not look or feel like it, but the end result is she's doing this for you, so she can be a better (wife, girlfriend, partner, companion) to you.

Don't expect change to happen overnight. Part of the problem is we live in a world of quick fixes and instant gratification. People have come to expect things to be easy, to right themselves with the swipe of a credit card, the popping of a pill, the immediacy of a text message. With PMDD, it doesn't work that way. With PMDD, your partner has to work doubly hard to be the change you both want to see in the world, because not only is she bumping up against the rest of the world, who most of the time is bumping back (to say the least), half the time she's fighting *herself.*

That same herself she needs to treat with kid gloves at times.

Managing a woman's PMDD is not easy, but it is possible. More than possible. But no pills are going to magically fix your partner's life. Only she can do that. Sure, she can do it with the aid of pharmaceuticals if she must, but even with anti-depressants, the end goal is for your partner to eventually stand on her own two feet.

So what about all this talk about brain chemistry and chemical imbalances? It's probably true, but not in the way the pharmaceutical companies would have us believe. There's a whole lot more to PMDD than just a simple chemical or hormonal imbalance, and we need to stop treating it like all women with PMDD need is a magic pill. Your partner is a whole person—mind, body, heart, and soul. Each and every one of us is. We're not just a categorized assortment of body parts our medical system has divided into specialties to treat independently of each other. The body works best when all the parts act together. In treating her PMDD, you need to look at the whole woman, not just one fragment of her hormonal system.

Keep in mind also that estrogen and progesterone might not be the only hormones involved in PMDD—they're simply the only ones being studied for PMDD at this time. Antidepressants and contraceptives (oral and long-acting reversible, or LARCs), are the two mainline medical treatments offered for PMDD. But using them is like shooting a cannon at a pigeon. A woman's neuro-endocrine system is delicate and individualized. These over-the-top drugs provided for PMDD merely blanket that complicated system. They don't get to the heart of the problem, because *nobody knows* what causes PMDD. It's been nearly seventy years since the first medical paper on PMS was published, and still nobody knows what causes it.

Meanwhile, millions of women have tried either or both current mainline treatment drugs, and several versions of each, with no relief, and quite often worsening of their symptoms. The anecdotal consensus at the first National Conference of the National Organization for PMDD was that in the long run these mainline treatments do not work. Many of these women had been on either birth control or antidepressants (or both) for PMDD for more than twenty years, with only short, intermittent periods of feeling well, if any.

What kind of woman survives twenty-plus years of solutions that didn't work?

Women with PMDD consider themselves weak. I think just the opposite. I think we are by far some of the strongest and most courageous women I have met. We're also very creative, resourceful, talented, and smart. And we are these things despite a medical system that works against us rather than for us.

To successfully manage our PMDD, we need to both learn how to navigate this medical system that isn't set up to help us, and to learn how to make our PMDD work *for* us, instead of against us.

That is the balance that needs to be corrected, and that correction will only come in time, and over time. A pill can't give your partner balance. All it can do is mask her symptoms and delay the process until she gets fed up with being overmedicated and (with your help) takes the steps she needs to take to determine what works best for *her* PMDD.

Chapter Two

———◆———

She Needs to Learn to Treat Herself Well

The most important thing for a woman with PMDD is to have a good relationship with herself. How she can accomplish this is covered in my book *PMDD and Relationships*. In this book for partners I wish to stay focused on what you, as her partner, can do to aid in her recovery from rampant PMDD.

First you must understand that women are socialized to put everybody else first. Love means doing for others. It's how we get love, how we give and show love, how we determine our worth in the world. Or at least that's what we're raised to believe. But the bible tells us to *Love your neighbor as yourself*.

Loving yourself is hard when you have PMDD. We do and say things we regret all the time. We also spend a *lot* of time beating ourselves up. So think, just think about all the good and positive things you and your partner with PMDD could be doing with that time and energy instead. What would happen if she just acknowledged her mistakes, did what she could to make amends, accepted that she'd done her best with the information she had at the time, and then got on with her life—your life, together?

Can you imagine how different your relationship would be?

So the first step to your partner's loving herself is to accept herself as she is, right here, right now. Is she in the middle of a bad episode, or is she doing well today? Is her day just so-so? That's fine, too. Start right where the two of you are. If she's having a bad day, what can you do right now to help her make *your day together* a little better? Maybe suggest that she put her feet up and take a little rest while you do whatever it was she was on her way to do? Maybe watch the kids so she can take a break and call a friend? Maybe offer some (good quality dark) chocolate? Give her some time to read? Maybe watch a movie with her? Maybe make her a cup of tea and let her just sit there feeling miserable for a while?

As partners, we don't like to see our other half in pain. But sometimes that's the best thing we can do...give them some down time to wallow in their misery for just a little while...and with time and patience they may well come to realize how blessed they are.

Nobody says we have to be happy all the time. I don't know anybody who is happy all the time. And there's nothing wrong with giving a woman a little down time, a little pampering, to help her get back on her feet again.

9

I have a real dislike for taking drugs. Any kind of drug. I'm all about natural health and healing. I'm especially against the unnecessary use of pain pills and antidepressants. But a friend once explained it to me this way: When you're in constant pain, when your body has gone haywire and is sending an uninterrupted stream of "I hurt" or "I feel miserable" signals to your brain, then what is the harm in taking an occasional pill to chemically interrupt that endless loop of biochemical messages running through your body? What's wrong with giving your body a little period of pain-free space to recover from that constant stream of pain messages circulating through your system?

Along those same lines, if your partner's pain is mental, as well as physical (and with PMDD it is), then what is the harm in her *briefly* taking an antidepressant to stop the endless loop of negative thoughts running through her brain? Just long enough to help her get back on her feet again.

Maybe six months to a year. Not for the rest of her life. Antidepressants and pain pills were never meant to be taken long-term or indefinitely. How they evolved into what they are today has more to do with market share than human health and wellness.

So, in the case of chronic **physical** pain, taking a pain pill can provide a small break in constant misery. Just enough time for your partner to catch her breath and remember what it feels like to feel good again, and marshal her resources for the next wave of pain.

In the case of **mental** pain, it's possible an antidepressant can provide a temporary break from that endless loop of negative thoughts in your partner with PMDD's head. Possible, but far from a sure thing, as antidepressants have been proven to work on a lot less people than both doctors and consumers have been led to believe. More than 50% of patients do not respond to antidepressants, other than to experience side effects. (And know this—studies have shown that intermittent use of antidepressants for PMDD (taken during the last two weeks of her cycle *only*) is more effective than continuous use of antidepressants for PMDD.)

In the case of **emotional** pain, encouraging her to talk to someone (a professional or friend), or pampering her in some way—listening to music, stroking a pet, reading a book, taking a walk, making a cup of hot cocoa—can give her that same little space between the endless loop of emotional pain she is feeling.

For spiritual pain, reading a book, watching a program, listening to a motivational CD, or going to a place of worship or time spent in silent prayer or contemplation can help. Giving her quiet time with the spirit inside.

Baby steps. Help her to take time out to get a handle on her pain, be it physical, mental, emotional, or spiritual. This is one of the greatest gifts you can offer the woman you love.

Since I started doing this unfailingly—listening to and attending to, instead of ignoring my body—I rarely have a PMDD episode to speak of. I've had a dip or two in mood that was quickly boosted by taking a walk and/or eating some protein and healthy whole-grain carbs (with five grams of sugar or less), but other than that my PMDD life has been on an even keel for several years now.

Loving ourselves comes from taking care of ourselves. From listening to ourselves and attending to our own needs. The more we do this, surprisingly enough, the *less* selfish we become. Because along the way, we manage to develop empathy, and realize we're not as alone in our pain as we thought we were.

So start small. Find just one way each day to help your partner with PMDD be good to herself. If you've read this far, you're the kind of partner who would do it for a friend who needs healing. Why not for her?

Chapter Three

―――◆―――

Snapping Out with PMDD

PMDD Flashback #1

As I said in the previous chapter, I am doing very well these days at managing my PMDD, but for the purposes of this book, to show you how I used to be, I will periodically include a story from my PMDD past. These stories come from blog posts written at the time, and often while under the influence of my PMDD.

〜〜

Snapping Out with PMDD

Here's but one small example of how PMDD can affect a relationship. A few weeks ago my teenage son mentioned a wildly popular movie he'd seen over the weekend, and asked if I wanted to watch it with him. I love watching movies, love spending time with my son. I was thrilled he'd thought enough of the movie (and me) to ask so even though I had already seen the movie years before and didn't particularly care for it, I said, "Sure, honey, we can watch it this weekend."

Ever since he started kindergarten, we've enjoyed Movie Night every Sunday evening as a way to settle in and prepare for the week to come. So he got the movie, and brought it home. A few days later, movie in hand, he asks, "Do you want to watch the movie now?"

And I snapped out on him and told him in no uncertain terms that I did not.

I don't recall doing it. This is not me. I mean, I've watched *Winnie the Pooh* and *Thomas the Tank Engine* and *Theodore the Tugboat* videos over and over and over again. I've seen most Disney animated DVDs at least twice, some several times. For a couple of years, I stopped what I was doing every afternoon to watch the Power Rangers.

I have watched a LOT of shows and movies I might not have felt like watching, but did so because they were age appropriate at the time.

But apparently I changed my mind this time, and I don't even remember doing so.

A few weeks later, I mentioned to my son in passing that we hadn't watched the movie yet, and he looked at me and said, "That's because you said, 'I don't see why I should have to sit through a movie I don't even like just because you want me to watch it.' "

"I did?" I asked, totally embarrassed. "When did I do that?"

"A few days after I first asked you about it and you said it would be okay."

"I'm sorry," I said. "I don't remember doing that. What did you say or do when I did that?"

He shrugged and said, "I just figured it was one of your PMDD days and left it alone."

I'm glad he knew it wasn't him that caused my snap-out, but still…

"Where's the movie now?" I asked.

"In my room," he says.

"You want to watch it?"

He did. We did. It was better than I remembered.

I try not to look back, but I wonder how many other opportunities like that I missed because of something sharp I said when I didn't mean to. Worse yet, I wonder how many times I hurt someone's feelings by snapping out and don't even remember it.

Because that's part of PMDD. We get irritable, we snap at people, and *don't realize we're doing it.* That's what those who do not have PMDD do not understand. We think we're behaving normally until something ugly happens, or someone who feels close enough to us or comfortable enough with us gently points out we may be having an episode. (Which nine times out of ten we will vehemently deny until we realize they are right. And even then we might still deny it, out of sheer embarrassment.)

Or, before we are aware that we have PMDD, our partners may be less gentle or understanding, and may simply shout, "What the hell is wrong with you?"

We don't know, (truly, we don't—another thing people who do not have PMDD find it impossible to believe). And if we don't get help, the relationship falls apart.

It takes two to make a relationship work and it takes two to bring one to an end. Know this: It isn't and wasn't completely her fault. When your partner with PMDD is having an episode of PMDD, certain factors are truly out of her control.

However, her PMDD is an explanation, not an excuse. (I will say this over and over and over again, because it is vital that both you and your partner understand this.) True, her rage and irritability and emotional outbursts during an episode of PMDD are as uncontrollable as an allergic reaction. That doesn't make them or the consequences from them any less painful, but neither does it mean she should drown herself in guilt afterward. She simply needs to apologize, do what she can to make up for it, and move on.

If you truly love your partner, you will understand and accept that there are times when she just isn't herself.

If she truly loves you, she'll do everything in her power to see that those episodes are few and far between.

Some may misinterpret my use of the word "love" in this section, thinking I mean "If you only love your partner enough..."

That is not what I am saying. My definition of love comes from the bible, 1 Corinthians 13: *Love is patient, love is kind. It does not envy, it does not boast, it is not proud. It is not rude, it is not self-seeking, it is not easily angered, it keeps no record of wrongs. Love does not delight in evil but rejoices with the truth. It always protects, always trusts, always hopes, always perseveres.*

Using that definition, can you now see how *each* of you working together (not just one of you working alone) for the benefit of the relationship can create a firm foundation for that relationship? A foundation that can withstand the ravages of PMDD.

Chapter Four

———◆———

A Perfect Storm of PMDD

PMDD Flashback #2

A Perfect Storm of PMDD

Unfortunately, I'm one of those atypical types who has my PMDD served up in three different courses, which is one reason it took me so long to get diagnosed. All the sites and information said specifically that for it to be PMDD all symptoms must abate at the onset of menses, or when your period begins.

But mine never did. Mine came in three separate stages. Which I finally learned is possible as well. God knew I'd been living it long enough—but to see it mentioned in a book? Finally, I could go to my doctor with confidence and get diagnosed.

I often compare my symptoms of PMDD to the course of a hurricane. Pre-menstrually is the building storm, the wind and the rain, with symptoms of irritability, edginess, an inexplicable, almost ravenous hunger, and cravings for salt and three specific foods—cheese, chocolate, and oranges. I have yet to figure out why, although occasionally I get glimmers of understanding and I am sure I will find the answer some day. But for now it's enough to know that that's what I crave, and when I find myself reaching for nothing but those three foods, I know a storm is about to blow in.

On my pre-period days I also get jittery, clumsy, confused, and distracted, unable to focus on any one task for any length of time. My handwriting even changes. Usually, it's comfortable, loose, flowing. When I'm having an episode of PMDD, it's spiky, jerky, and messy. At times it looks like the handwriting of a much older woman. I'm always startled to see it come out that way, but not totally surprised, because as I'm writing my hand doesn't seem to work properly—which science has shown also accounts for my tendency to drop things more than usual during those periods of time.

Anyway, the unfamiliar handwriting is one clue that something is happening in my brain. My typing is also affected. I have a friend who pointed out that I don't bother to capitalize in my emails when I am having an episode of PMDD and I don't do a lot of smiley faces. It's as if to do either would take too much effort.

So in my case first comes the storm of irritability, anger, and rage. Snapping out at the drop of a hat. Lashing out at someone who didn't say anything out of the ordinary, but just struck me as wrong. Feeling under attack and wanting to hit someone, anyone. Just give me a chance. Not a reason, but a chance. I call these my wanting to "drink, smoke, and be bad" days. Impulsive behavior does its best to take over, and I can fully understand in those days why some women go out and do completely irresponsible things they later regret. I've felt like doing so more times than I can count, and have complete empathy for those who give in to these bizarre urges. If I didn't have a core of faith inside me that keeps me anchored in good times and bad, I would go out and do the same.

Usually the worst thing I ever did was go shopping and buy all sorts of things I didn't need or never wore. If I were to look at my credit card statements for those time periods I'm sure I would see a pattern of spending that coincides with the pre-menstrual portion of my PMDD episodes. Fortunately, now I understand what is happening and stay home on those days instead of going shopping. Because inevitably the bill would come, and I would wonder why on earth I had done such a thing.

When I worked as an analyst for the government, on my pre-menstrual days I would suddenly notice that I hadn't received a response on this project or the other, and would call up the parties in question and remind them I was waiting to hear from them. On any other day it wouldn't have bothered me. People get busy, people go on vacation, people have priorities, people forget. In the overall scheme of things, my projects were never that vital. Most of the time, I was tolerant and flexible.

But on a PMDD day, everyone I came across was either incompetent or personally holding me back from untold success.

I might not rant at them directly—after all, even on my worst days I knew you catch more flies with honey than vinegar—but I would complain to anyone else who would listen about how I seemed to be the only person around who could get things done and do them right. I had no tolerance for the slightest delay or mistake.

Then my period would come and I'd be miserable in a new way for a couple of days. Cramps, backaches, and pain that sometimes radiated as far down as my knees, and made me feel like I wanted to throw up. Breathing hurt. I would lie very still, hot pack pressed to my lower abdomen, which felt like someone was slowly trying to pull my insides out with a three-pronged gardening tool. Every. Single. Month.

That, if you want to believe it, was the eye of the hurricane. The first two days of my period.

Then the sadness kicked in. On Day 3. Always on Day 3. If it was going to come, that would be the day. It didn't always come, still doesn't. Now I know it has to do with whether I release an egg or not that month. No egg, no sadness. Woo hoo! Party time.

Not quite. But at least it's a lot more pleasant around here when the sadness doesn't come. Because when it does, I'm tired all the time, my head feels like it has an iron band around it, and I sigh a lot—big, deep sighs like the weight of the world is on my shoulders—because for me, it is. Most everything looks hopeless, every good idea I had during the month goes to shit, I want to weep at every turn, you don't dare tell me a joke or tease me, and I spend a lot of time wondering why I even bother.

During this phase of my PMDD, I used to beat myself up incessantly over the people I had snapped out at the week before. Now, at least, I don't do that anymore. I know I didn't mean it, and in most cases it doesn't get that far anymore, because I have a much deeper awareness of what is going on and can catch myself in counterproductive behavior.

Now, when I catch myself starting to snap out, I apologize and explain I am having a bad day. Most of my friends know what that means. If the person isn't my friend, it's okay to leave it at an apology without an explanation. Never ruin a perfectly good apology with an explanation. You don't need to justify yourself or your behavior. You only need to acknowledge it, apologize for it if the incident warrants an apology, and move on.

But back then, as I said, I would beat myself up incessantly. This only intensified my sadness and made me feel like a totally worthless human being. My friends couldn't possibly be my friends. They wouldn't be my friends if they knew the real me. How would I ever find anybody to love me if I was so impossible to be around? Yada yada yada. You know how it goes.

The bottom line is the first part of my personal hurricane is the moody, bitchy, out of control part. Then would come the eye of the storm and two days of solid pain but surprisingly clear thinking. Fortunately, now, as I begin to enter menopause, it's just the clear thinking part, and a huge surge of positive energy. It's a definite reprieve in the storm.

Then the sadness comes. Dysphoria. The first D in PMDD. My depression. Or The Fog, as I call it. Back then it was devastating. How could anybody not hate me? Now I am able to separate myself from it and while it is still not pleasant, I know I am not my depression. I rest, relax, take it easy, spend time reading or listening to music or doing something quiet and non-demanding, secure in the knowledge that my PMDD will pass. I do what I can to help it pass sooner. I take walks, take naps, eat right and take supplements. I do not allow my negative thoughts to take over. In fact, I smile at them, knowing I know better. God does love me and so do the people in my life. My ideas are good ones and I am full of creativity. I am strong, capable, and competent. I'm just running a little slower than usual today. Just a tad off my stride. It will pass and I will be fine.

And I am. One day The Fog lifts, and it's back to the hectic pace of my life as usual—until the next wave of cravings and irritability hits.

Chapter Five

————◆————

Comments from Readers

A Perfect Storm of PMDD is one of my most popular blog posts. Occasionally, readers leave comments. The following are snippets of comments made after I wrote this post. I thought I'd share a random few here so you get a chance to hear from somebody besides me. Any responses to the reader from me are in italics.

————

With everything I've been going through these past few years and it getting worse and worse since the birth of my second son almost 4 years ago, I've been searching and searching for an explanation. I thought I'd found it in PMDD until I read that symptoms go away once your period starts. Not my case, just like you. I also start with anger and irritability and intolerance to noise and then things calm down once my period starts, but I'm exhausted. Then, 3 or 4 days after it begins, I get one day period-free then the next day, it starts up again with first-day cramps and back pain. Sadness and depression are present throughout at varying intensity. So basically, I'm myself for about a week and a half, two weeks out of every month. The rest of the time I'm this sort of monster, feeling worthless and useless, feeling like I'm a bad mother and an awful girlfriend.

~·⁄·~

Thank you so much for giving me hope, 30 years of the same kind of PMDD as you describe. Am also drug free for ten years after being used as a human guinea pig by so-called professionals. Being told there is no such thing as PMDD, at the same time giving me coils that release hormones, hormone replacement therapy and SSRI's at the same time.

~·⁄·~

I have no close friends; most people think I am crazy and when I try to explain to them I sound even crazier. So I live in isolation mostly and have to pretend I am okay when I see people. My mother has tried to have me admitted a few times. Only my son and daughter get the real me and my PMDD and if it was not for them I am sure I would have taken my own life by now. Thank you so much, you make me feel like holding on and living.

~·⁄·~

My heart goes out to all of you going through PMDD. You are not alone. Mine got to a point where it was affecting all my body systems. For a week and a half my body did shut down and all I could do was sleep. I even

25

ended up in the emergency room with a twisted bowel and I suspect it had to do with PMDD because the doctors failed to figure out why my bowel twisted. Imagine, during PMDD, I actually forget how to spell words, my cognitive skills dropped to zero ... I burst into tears when I read everyone's story because I know what PMDD can do.

~·~

I love the name Livingonaprayer. If it weren't for that I don't know where I'd be. I also find that my PMDD continues through my period. No major pain except for extreme achiness in my joints, almost as if my bones hurt in my legs. I also find that on around day two or three I have heightened sensitivity to sound, smell, and touch. The next day is usually a total crash. I am so tired I can barely function.

~·~

I know the feeling of the storm—the mental confusion and the lack of patience. I could snap at anybody for the slightest thing which is very odd because I am usually extremely passive. But I have thought the same thing, "God help anyone who messes with me at this time." It's kinda scary to think I could do something I would later regret but as the site says—we are living on a prayer.

~·~

I don't know if I am the only man reading these blogs, but my girlfriend's PMDD has been quite a rollercoaster ride in our relationship of 3 1/2 yrs. Obviously it must be awful for her, but it certainly has put a huge strain on our relationship. She is very intelligent, beautiful, etc, and within 9 months of meeting I had proposed, just after she moved in with me. The monthly PMDD became so bad with talking about weddings etc that I eventually said I thought we should delay the wedding. Well, that created so many more problems. I didn't want to let her down, but her behavior took me by surprise every month, and I was left astounded at what had just happened.

～ιㅑㅌ

I am at the beginning of my journey to understand my PMDD. About 2, 3 years ago I started noticing my unexplainable bouts of depression had a pattern. Unfortunately I had no one around who had ever heard of PMDD but a couple of months ago my ob/gyn diagnosed me with PMDD and it's helped a lot. I'm in between testing Prozac and 5-HTP separately on myself to see if one will help as they cannot be taken together.

～ιㅑㅌ

My wife has PMDD 2 weeks each month. I can now track it on a calendar. The meanness, sharp tongue, irritability, over sensitivity to the slightest comment...it's all there each month, like clockwork. I used to make the mistake of reacting to her negativity, which results in a showdown at the OK Corral with talks of divorce, etc. etc. Now, I just keep my mouth shut, offer my help, not reacting to the negativity. It's not easy at all. My only escape is to go to the gym when it seems everything I do is wrong in her eyes. But I bear it each month because I love my wife and I know it's not her. I say she becomes Mr. Hyde once a month for 2 weeks, and I just learn to keep my mouth shut. A big exercise in tolerance and patience. If you love your wife or special someone, tolerance and patience are vital. If you don't have them, you will suffer.

~\l/~

I may also suffer from anxiety separate from PMDD and sometimes I cannot escape those terrifying feelings of no control … I'm so afraid of those who think its PMS because my only defense is "No, it's different, far more intense." "Yeah, that's what each woman says about their period." "No, really, I consider suicide once a month like clockwork, and that's not normal." "Oh, more drama…" These are conversations I've had and fear I'll have again.

~\l/~

PMS is primarily physical symptoms with a little moodiness thrown in. PMDD is something else entirely. You can't be responsible for what other people think, but given the responses you presented in your comment, my guess is they simply don't care enough (or have the skills required) to "listen" to you. The fault does not lie with you. You are attempting to communicate your condition and your needs. They are not listening.

~\l/~

My girlfriend would storm out over the smallest of things, and I wouldn't see her for a week. It would then take us another week to make up, by which time her next cycle would start. I ended up losing 2 well paid jobs because of all of the problems we had. We are still together, but live separately, and are trying to work things

out. I know how hard it is for her, and she is my main concern, but it has also really affected me. I think our only long term solution is for her to have children, and then have a hysterectomy. Identical story to her mother.

~⋅ᴵ⋅~

Is there any way to get this corrected, I am on the pill but it does not help; around that time I get psycho crazy and my husband and my fighting gets bad. I do not want my kids going through a broken home because of this. I am so torn up and do not know what to do.

~⋅ᴵ⋅~

Footnote:

The Strange Case of Dr. Jekyll and Mr. Hyde is a novella written in 1886 by Robert Louis Stevenson. According to Wikipedia, the work is commonly associated with the mental condition often called "split personality," referred to in psychiatry as Dissociative Identity Disorder, where within the same body there exists more than one distinct personality. In this case, there are two personalities in Dr. Jekyll, one apparently good and the other evil; with completely opposite levels of morality. The novella has since become a part of the language, with the phrase "Dr. Jekyll and Mr. Hyde" referring to a person who is vastly different in moral character from one situation to the next.

Chapter Six

———— ◆ ————

Relationships with Friends

Next, I'm going to talk about relationships with friends. I know everybody wants to get right to the part about Relationships with Partners, but really, any relationship you have with a partner, fiancé, spouse, boyfriend, girlfriend or any kind of significant other should be rooted in friendship for the best chance to succeed. If you're already in a relationship, you might still want to read this section, especially if the foundation of that relationship is crumbling and you need to start building it back up again.

∿

Choosing Our Friends Wisely - Whether We Have PMDD Or Not

Let's talk about friendships. Those of us with PMDD have at one time or another isolated ourselves, because we don't feel friends or family will "understand" when we are having an episode, so it's easier just to go into isolation and deal with it alone.

Easier, but is it healthier? Wouldn't it be nice for her to know she's still loved and people still want to be around her, even when she feels the most unlovable?

She does this by choosing her friends wisely. She does this by choosing friends who are patient, kind, compassionate, and understanding. She does this by moving away from people who are not. As women with PMDD, we need to look out for ourselves, because—nobody, no matter how much they love us—is going to do it for us. If this means ending or scaling back a few friendships and/or relationships, then so be it.

Why would we want to remain in a friendship/relationship that isn't healthy for us?

Your partner with PMDD needs to decide who she wants to have in her life, and who she doesn't. Who adds stress to it, and who doesn't. This will determine who she should see less often, speak/email/text less often, or speak to only when they run into each other during school, church, or social events....

The last thing your partner with PMDD needs is to keep company with anyone who has shown her anger, annoyance, or impatience due to her PMDD, or indicated they think less of her when she had to cancel an outing due to her PMDD. Or worse, someone who minimizes her efforts to attend events *despite* her PMDD.

For that, she needs to be celebrated, not castigated.

I am not saying you need to create a spoiled princess here. I am asking you, as her partner, to appreciate the enormous amount of effort it takes to simply "show up" some days when you are having an episode of PMDD. Why this is so difficult, I will get into later.

So please encourage your partner with PMDD to surround herself with the kind of person she would like to be. In my case, that's kind, caring, giving, compassionate, and loving. I've moved away from anyone who doesn't embody the kind of qualities I want to see more of in my life. I've moved away from those who are negative, demeaning, demanding, needy, and live lives full of drama they create themselves.

Some people need a lot of drama in their lives to be happy. I'm not one of them.

I have many different friends, with all sorts of different lifestyles, problems, interests, and beliefs—but they all hold the same caring qualities in common. They have patience and understanding, tolerance and compassion, and accept when I tell them I'm having an episode and can't really participate in whatever is going on.

The same goes for my husband.

They all allow me to talk about my PMDD openly, and even though they don't understand it, and cannot imagine what I am going through, they accept that I am going through something that is extremely painful, upsetting, and draining for me.

They don't try to:
> Talk me out of it
>
> Tell me to get over it
>
> Tell me I'm being a bitch or boring or no fun to be around
>
> Blame me for ruining their day or plans

Nor do they tell me to "smile," "relax," "shape up," or "stop being so sensitive."

And nobody, but nobody, tells me to "just think happy thoughts."

My husband and friends let me be quiet when I need to be quiet, and understand if I say things that don't quite make sense.

On my part, I feel it's up to me not to snap at or lash out at my friends and family, and so I take full responsibility for that. If I slip, I apologize immediately, and explain that I am having a PMDD day.

PMDD is an explanation, but never an excuse.

In this way I have, over time, created a circle of friends who might not fully understand what PMDD is about, but respect and understand that *I know* what's going on, and if I say I'm having a bad day, then they accept that I am having a bad day, and don't expect or ask for more than I am able to give.

My life is very good. I have been abundantly blessed in ways tangible and intangible. I have a fully supportive family, caring and understanding friends, a warm and comfortable home, work that fulfills me, and a son who has been well-trained to deal with a woman's hormonal moods—while at the same time accepting no disrespect from me or any other woman because of those moods.

I didn't always have these things. I've been working at it for over fifteen years, slowly pruning away what (and who) no longer needs to be a part of my life, and moving into the forefront of my life what needs to stay for me to live the kind of life I want to live—calm, creative, fulfilling, and productive.

I lost touch with some friends along the way. But as I began to better understand **and accept** myself and my PMDD limitations, I gained new, more accepting and understanding friends. I also reconnected with some of my original friends in ways I never expected, while others came and went with the ebb and flow of life.

Studies show that if you hang around certain kinds of people, you will become more like them. If you surround/align yourself with hard workers, you'll work harder; if you surround yourself with positive people, you'll be more positive; if you hang with those who take an active part in maintaining their health and wellness, you'll be more active and healthier overall; if you keep company with goal-oriented people, you'll attain a few goals yourself.

In general, if you hang around successful people, you'll be more successful. At whatever you try.

The flip side of that works as well: if you surround yourself with complainers, you'll complain more; if you surround yourself with people who like to overindulge in food, drink, toxic environments or substances; you'll do more of the same. If you hang with people who do things you know are harmful to your health and wellness, *you will do more harmful things than you may personally want to*, just to fit in.

So do what you can to support your partner with PMDD in choosing the people she wants to spend her time with. If you want her to be well, then make friends as a couple with those who are also trying to be well. Think about it, and then adjust your life together accordingly.

Help her to listen to her body, notice how she feels before, during, or after she's around certain people. Some people can churn you up just thinking about being around them. Take time to notice who these people are in your partner's life. Help her to sort through her feelings about these people if she will let you. Don't just go through life on autopilot, accepting whatever comes your way.

Slow down, come to know yourself and your partner better, make friends with each other, become best friends if you are not already, accept that she has PMDD, and then choose the rest of your friends wisely.

One small step at a time.

Chapter Seven

——◆——

How to Survive Family Gatherings Together

Relationships - How To Survive Family Gatherings

There are a lot of us who genuinely would like to get along with our families and have our family gatherings filled with happy memories of good times shared. There are also a lot of us, who, for one reason or another, aren't willing or ready to make any sort of break with our fundamental family ties—because without family, what are we, but alone?

Nobody likes to be alone. Especially on the holidays, when according to what we see on television, everyone else is having the time of their lives.

So in this section I want to offer some ideas for things you can do to make your family gatherings, be they over the holidays or for any family occasion, a little more pleasant for both you and your partner with PMDD, especially if she is in PMDD mode.

1. **Lower your expectations.** Most people go into the holidays with Norman Rockwell expectations and end up deeply disappointed, even depressed and suicidal. Where do most of these expectations come from? The media. Starting as early as September, advertisements abound showing happy families sharing holiday joy. So don't blame yourself—or your partner with PMDD—if your holiday event falls short of the idealized version you see on TV. This is tantamount to blaming yourself for not having a body as hot as your favorite movie star's. Looking good is what they get paid to do. If you got paid to look that good, you would, too.

So don't fall for the hype. Work with what you have, and stop trying to imitate some marketing specialist's unrealistic image of what *your* holiday gathering should be like. For instance, for Thanksgiving two years ago my husband and I tried out a new recipe for veggie chili, made cornbread, bought some ice cream, invited one (one!) friend over, and had a great time. This same friend and I used to do the whole turkey dinner thing with a big group of friends, which was fun at the time, but then she and I shifted to more low key activities.

For Christmas, we went our separate ways. No harm, no foul. For Easter, my husband and I spent the weekend in a lakeside cabin with different friends, from my high school.

It's all good, as long as it works for *your* relationship.

2. **Arrive determined to look for the positive throughout the day.** If someone brings up a topic you'd rather

not discuss, just say, "I really haven't thought much about that lately." Then excuse yourself to head off for the food and or drink table, maybe ask if there is anything you can bring back for them. (If you're already at the table, pick up the nearest serving dish and offer some food. "Would you like some more mashed potatoes?" Switch the focus to them, in a polite, non-threatening way.) Once you've returned with whatever they might have asked for, offer a pleasant "Here you go," and then be on your way. Either way, the uncomfortable topic has been diverted.

3. **Use the event as an opportunity for growth as a couple.** Practice the skills of patience, kindness, tolerance, acceptance, and/or self-control. Congratulate yourself every time you manage to take the high road and not take the bait from the person trying to get you (or especially your partner with PMDD) to lose your (her) cool, either deliberately or inadvertently. One of the best books I've read that has to do with dealing with difficult people is *Thank You for Being Such a Pain,* by Mark Rosen. Use the occasion as an opportunity to learn about how and who you "don't" want to be. Help your partner to be who she wants to be. Don't just ignore her to fend for herself at the event.

4. **Do everything in your power to get a good night's sleep beforehand**. This goes double for your partner, as stress fuels PMDD just as much as PMDD creates stress. A woman with PMDD needs to arrive at every event feeling well-rested, comfortable, calm, and secure. If your partner is feeling none of these things on the date of the event, or the opposite of these things, then she is *not wrong in wanting to cancel*, and if she does,

please do not try to make her feel guilty or in any way defective or "less than" for doing so.

Would you stay home if you had the flu? An episode of PMDD is a hotbed of negativity. Negative moods are just as contagious as the flu and can ruin a party just as easily. By staying away from the event, your partner is not being selfish and uncaring—she is in essence protecting the event, while also taking care of herself. This is exactly what a woman with PMDD needs to do during an episode of PMDD.

5. **Eliminate three words from your vocabulary for the day — Always, Never, and Ever.** Try it. Practice with your partner in advance. As in so many other areas, awareness is the key. Become more aware of these "conflict coals" and do your best to not add any more to the fire. Or, as an exercise in self-entertainment, notice how often others use these coals of conflict to fan the flames of family discontent.

6. **Stay sober.** I know this is a hard one, because a lot of people use alcohol to get through the day, thinking it's the only way they will be able to deal with it, but in truth alcohol only contributes to the problem, because it magnifies whatever issues are already on the table, or lurking just beneath the surface. Besides, a woman with PMDD needs to stay away from alcohol. Like stress and trauma and abuse, alcohol only makes PMDD symptoms worse. If your partner with PMDD must drink, downing a full glass of water in between each alcoholic beverage would both hydrate her and pace her alcohol consumption.

7. **Don't choose sides in any conflict that develops.** Period.

8. **Stay away from discussions involving sex, politics, and religion.** If you are not successful, congratulate yourself for at least having the willingness to try.

9. **Invite a friend or two** who has nowhere else to go for the holiday dinner. Sometimes bringing new people into the situation will help to keep unruly relatives on their best behavior. Or will at least make them consider restraining themselves in the presence of guests.

10. **Drive separately, so your partner can escape if need be.**

11. Another sanity-saving option is to **arrive late and leave early.** Limit your time with your relatives so that whichever of the above you might be willing to try has a bigger chance of success.

12. **When all else fails, disengage.** Because sometimes nothing less than to Just Say No will do. Plan an alternate holiday gathering/event and proceed with it guilt-free, telling your family you're taking a break and will see them next time around.

For if awareness is the first step, and it is, shedding guilt and blame is the second. The book, *Guilt is the Teacher, Love is the Lesson*, by Dr. Joan Borysenko is an excellent resource for helping you, and especially your partner, to do just that.

Chapter Eight

———◆———

General Wrap-up on Relationships
(before we start getting specific)

It's Not Personal, It's Just Your PMDD

Stress at home is bad enough, but for a woman with PMDD, it can be the key element that prevents her from getting well, as any kind of trouble at home only exacerbates her PMDD symptoms. During a PMDD episode, women with PMDD are biologically sensitive creatures, and can be sensitive to light, sound, touch, taste, and smells. This has been clinically proven. A PMDD-ing woman's five senses can be enhanced during an episode, enhanced to the point of physical discomfort and beyond, which makes us react in ways not welcome or understood by those who do not suffer such on again, off again changes in sensitivity to our senses.

Please understand this: It's biological, this shift/change that happens in our bodies, but we react to it/manifest it emotionally.

Anger has been a basic form of self defense since the cave dwellers. Our bodies are hardwired to react with some form of flight or fight (including anger and aggression) when we feel threatened.

Kids too loud? You snap and snarl to get them to quiet down. But what happens when your partner with PMDD's head is pounding with a PMDD migraine, and she tells you to shut up and turn out the lights. Both of these reactions are nothing more than self-preservation instincts kicking in. Too many flashing lights? Too much electronic noise? Same deal. You giving her a hard time? Asking for something she can't provide in that moment?

Her biological responses kick in, and she lashes out in self defense.

You respond with "What's wrong with you? I was just…"

You wonder if she's crazy. Why? Because she's out of control.

But PMDD is biological in nature, and deals with, among other things, her stress responses. The only thing she or you can do to break the cycle (short of taking drugs) is to help her to get to know herself as well as you possibly can, and together learn ways to head off any of her "natural as an allergic reaction" responses to stress.

If you chart her symptoms, which is a must for a woman with PMDD, you can tell when things are going to start getting dicey in your life. You can plan around those days, and help her to plan to take it easy on those days if at all possible. Help her to pamper herself a little. You can also warn those you live with that those days are coming.

My house is a haven. It's where I go to find peace, to recharge, to rest and relax. It wasn't always that way, and I had to make some difficult choices and changes to get to where I am today. One baby step at a time.

But now, if I am having a bad day, all I have to do is say so, and everyone knows it has nothing to do with them and everything to do with me and my PMDD. The best course of action is to avoid me, make no demands, agree with me if I start something, and not take anything I say or do personally.

That does not absolve me of any responsibility.

My job is to 1) stay aware of what I am doing, 2) go about my business quietly, 3) gently remind people who ask for something I can't give at that moment that I am having a bad day, 4) do my best not to start anything, and 5) not take anything personally.

The best advice for *everyone* involved is to not take anything personally.

Your partner needs to know that this is not a license for her to freely do and say whatever she wants to during an episode, but an agreement that if things should go south or get out of hand—it's not personal. It's just her PMDD.

When it comes to kids, it should be easy to simply explain to them that Mommy is having a bad day and needs some quiet time, and it would be a really big help if they could find something quiet to do while Mommy rests so she can feel better sooner.

If your kids don't understand or refuse to honor this simple request, then a parenting class might be in order. There's nothing wrong with asking for a little peace and quiet, a little time to regroup, especially when you are not feeling well.

Around here, we use code phrases like…

I'm feeling fragile today.

I can't handle any new information today.

I'm having a bad day.

I'm having a sad day.

Whatever you say or do today will be wrong, so it's best to steer clear of me.

It's not personal.

It's not you.

All I want is chocolate.

Let's go out to eat.

I can't stay awake today.

I think I'll just read a book for a while.

I can't seem to hold onto my thoughts today.

When all else fails, I call an end to my day and go to bed. So when your PMDD-ing woman goes to bed, especially alone, try not to feel hurt or abandoned. Consider that it might be to protect what she loves the most; you, and her family.

Chapter Nine

More Reader Comments

These are in regard to my blog post It's Not Personal, It's Just Your PMDD. Any responses from me are in italics.

This is SUCH good advice! Thank you for continuing to give encouragement and suggestions for how to help, other than pushing meds that do exactly what you said - create side effects to add onto the stress one is already dealing with! If anyone has an iPhone, I would highly recommend the P tracker. I've dealt with PMDD for almost 6 years now and until now never tracked my symptoms, I just know when my "off" days are going to be and when I'm most likely to have an episode. But with this app, you can chart your symptoms and write notes—

help yourself remember what is going on around you. It's a great tool!!!

～✶～

Oh, but this is so true. The "what's the matter with you?" question is like a red flag to a bull, because, let's face it, how many days of the month do you accommodate the people around you, mood swings, demands, stresses and all, before your hormones dictate that you take care of "you" and snap?

～✶～

This post comes at an apt time. Was met with "I know you feel like crap, but you don't need to be mean to me, you're not even trying today, I want to hear that you're trying."

～✶～

This, my PMDD friends, is emotional manipulation. The partner is asking for something the woman is clearly not capable of giving at that moment. He speaks to her as if he is training a dog. And below, she first accepts the blame for his behavior, then realizes she is not entirely at fault here. Yay, you!

～✶～

I was trying SO hard it was a tough day and my 'reaction' was VERY minor in the grand scheme of things. But then I realized later he was bringing his own frustrations with him because of other circumstances. It's not always you...other people have tough days too.

～✶～

I want to thank you for bringing rationality to something that is so inherently irrational. For the past

two years, I've been coping with the realization that my life-long "insanity" is PMDD. All this time, I've been single. Now, I've met someone new and have not yet told him the "evil truth." Your blog is fantastic and really helps me to understand how to approach my new situation with this someone special. Thank you.

~\⁄~

I am for sure bookmarking your site. I have been living with this since I was 11 years old. It gets worse when my life tends to be more stressful. I am just beginning to learn about PMDD. I believe I was mistakenly diagnosed with depression when I was 12 and mistakenly diagnosed with PCOS in my 20's. *[Polycystic Ovarian Syndrome]* I am now 33 and have had to have physical therapy for stress-related pain. It's all related to PMDD.

~\⁄~

I've spent the last 4 hours crying off and on and arguing with my boyfriend while trying to explain to him that I just needed someone to talk to. PMDD is such a lonely disorder. Its rarity coupled with its extreme nature make it so difficult to cope with at times. I can't just talk to other women because in reality most of them haven't experienced this. My boyfriend keeps comparing it to PMS and he tries to make me feel better by saying all women go through it, but he is completely off base and misinformed. It is not PMS and most women don't go through this.

~\⁄~

The thing I struggle with the most in my relationships is trying to convince people that I'm aware of my symptoms, but I can't control them. I can't simply will it all away. I have actually chosen to take an anti-anxiety drug during the luteal phase of my menstrual cycle. I have downloaded the WomanLog [calendar Android] app on my phone that helps me track my cycle. The drug helps tremendously, but since I only take them 2 weeks out of every month, I always have to wait 48 hours from taking the first pill for them to kick in with relief.

⁓

If you are already tracking your cycle, and know when your period will arrive, why not start taking your anti-anxiety meds a day or two sooner? Don't wait for the symptoms to present themselves. Head them off at the pass!

⁓

Prior to my diagnosis and treatment I attempted suicide once and threatened suicide at least 4 other times.

⁓

I am embarrassed to admit that I have this illness to anyone as only two people in my life know that I suffer...my mom and my boyfriend. My mom is very supportive, but my boyfriend treats me like I am weak-minded. I'm not sure our relationship will survive this.

⁓

I'm afraid to date anyone else for fear that no one will ever accept this about me.

⁓

I feel hopeful at least that if I can encourage my boyfriend to become educated about what I am experiencing and how to better support me, then perhaps we can make it. I pray that one day he will realize when it comes to my PMDD, I don't want his opinion, I just want his love and support.

～ﾉﾚ～

I have been suffering from PMDD for what seems 3 years after beginning birth control. Once I stopped birth control last year, it has been a roller coaster as the monthly mood swings have been amped to full extent. I am screaming like a banshee, crying, throwing things, etc. and I can honestly say I sit back as if paralyzed and [horrified] in my own mind, trying to break free from the cycle of Jekyll and Hyde.

～ﾉﾚ～

I usually like things neat and in order (kind of a perfectionist) on a normal basis and it seems it becomes tenfold when I am in the PMDD zone. I want everything to be finished properly, no loose ends, or else.

～ﾉﾚ～

PMDD truly puts much stress on our relationship. My boyfriend is usually sweet and apologetic, trying to solve things before they get out of control and I, of course, want things to go my way. If they don't, hell will literally break loose. Sometimes I don't even feel it coming on and I will just turn into a ball of negativity and I can`t seem to tell myself to stop. It is as if I am in a trance, and

everyone around me has the problem (I know, clearly the PMDD talking).

⚜

I used to be a perfectionist, too, and while still working a full time job, would think everyone else was completely inept during my monthly time. How could I be surrounded by such pervasive incompetence and inefficiency? The world was filled with idiots. On my PMDD days, it still is.

Chapter Ten

Are You the Right Partner?

Okay, now we're going to get into what I had in mind when I first thought about writing *PMDD and Relationships,* the companion book that covers this same material, but speaks to both women with PMDD and their partners.

The bottom line is we can have all kinds of relationships with all kinds of people, but how many of them are truly successful? How many of them make us smile instead of sigh or groan? How many would we rather not have?

A woman with PMDD needs to know:

1. Who lifts her spirit, and who tries to kill it?

2. Who treats her with respect and dignity, and who ignores and steamrolls over her?

3. Who takes care of her, and who takes away from her? I'm not just talking about time, energy, and money. I'm talking who are her emotional vampires?

4. Who would drain her dry if she'd let them?

5. Who cheers her on in life, and who drags her down?

6. Who is there for her, and who is not?

In short, who treats her like she matters to them, and who doesn't?

And where do you fall on the scale of things?

Are her boundaries clear, as to what she will and will not do or accept? If not, there is no way anyone can respect those boundaries. People are not mind readers.

How does she know what her boundaries are? She takes the time to get to know herself, her likes and dislikes, tastes and preferences, and what she will and will not tolerate. If she doesn't know herself in this way, or doesn't understand herself at all, how can she explain her PMDD to you, or anyone else?

Face it, most of us treat friends better than we do ourselves. We're there for friends, but when it comes to being there for ourselves, for any number of reasons we drop the ball. Why? Many of us have children, children who depend on us to be there for them, no matter what kind of day we are having. But taking care of ourselves first, seeing to our own health and wellness helps us to be better able to take care of them. When we're calm, relaxed, rested, and happy, we're much better able to provide that emotional stability our children need to grow into happy, well-adjusted adults.

To have a good relationship, we need a supportive partner. Period. If our partner isn't supportive of our needs as a woman with PMDD, we might as well be salmon swimming upstream. But for our partner to be supportive of those needs, we have to first know what those needs are.

This is where you, the partner comes in. When your partner with PMDD is having an episode, does she need calm and quiet, or does she need to be held? Does she need to be left alone, or does she want someone who can help to ease her out of her negative mood? Will flowers and candy help? Does she just want to watch TV or read a book, or does she want to talk?

The answers are as varied as can be. But the key to any good relationship is communication. Maybe one month she'll want to go out to dinner. Maybe another she'll want to take a long bath. Maybe she'll want to make some popcorn and watch a comedy. Maybe she'll want to go for a walk. Maybe she'll need a nap.

Maybe she just wants to feel appreciated.

Whatever she wants, she needs to be able to communicate that to you, her partner, *during her non-PMDD times,* so that you have an idea of what to do when she is in the PMDD zone.

Once you have a reasonable expectation of what her PMDD pattern is, you can prepare yourself for the bad days coming, and offer her some extra consideration on those days. If you have a really good relationship, you might be able to see the storm coming before it arrives. Years ago, there were times I was completely unaware that I was starting to act out of character, until a good friend pointed it out. Then I had to decide if he was right or not, because nobody knows my mental, emotional, or physical state as well as I do.

Sometimes my friend was right, and sometimes he was wrong. When he was right, we'd go into PMDD mode. When he was wrong, I would do my best to figure out what was really bothering me, and if he was involved, we would talk about it. If he wasn't, we either dropped the subject—because I like to figure things out on my own—or I would ask for advice in how to deal with the person or situation causing my anger and/or tears.

Never tell your partner she must be having an episode because she's upset with you for one reason or another. There are times in *everyone's* lives when we are genuinely angry or upset with someone about something. Anger and emotional upset are normal emotions and natural signals that something is not going right in our lives. They're like warning lights, flashing to let us know that "something is going on here" that needs to be addressed.

The key is to know the difference—is she genuinely angry, or has her PMDD kicked in?

If her PMDD has kicked in, revert to your list of code phrases I mentioned in Chapter Eight. Make up your own list. Agree on your PMDD code phrases beforehand, when she is feeling healthy and well. Then, when the bad days come, you will both be prepared and will have them ready to diffuse tense situations that arise.

A good relationship of any kind is based on mutual admiration and respect. If you're in a good relationship, you will respect your partner's need for space or extra help or attention when the bad days come. If you're not, you will likely find yourself with a partner who refuses to acknowledge that she has

PMDD—and that is another problem entirely. Partners like that only add to the problem, because they create stress for both of you, and anyone else in the household. Stress exacerbates PMDD, so yes, a woman's home environment does have a huge impact on her PMDD and ability to reach wellness.

The absolute, positive best thing you can do for your relationship is *do not add stress* when your partner is already stressed from within. If your partner won't cooperate in keeping her own stress level down, then there is more going on in your relationship than her PMDD. As I have said before, it takes two to make a relationship, and two to break it. If you're trying, and your partner isn't—again, it's not just about PMDD. In this case, she is using her PMDD as an excuse to avoid looking at whatever else may be going wrong in the relationship.

It's true...either one of you can make her PMDD a scapegoat for your relationship issues. It happens more often than not.

But remember, PMDD is an explanation, not an excuse.

For either one of you.

Chapter Eleven

———•———

Advice for Partners of Women with PMDD

Dealing With PMDD - Advice for Men

I've spent quite a bit of time searching the internet for resources and advice for men dealing with a woman who suffers from PMDD. Unfortunately, most articles casually lump PMS and PMDD together, which does a great disservice to both women with PMDD and their partners. In the comment sections of these articles both men and women express anger and resentment toward women who experience true PMDD; the men claiming the articles give women a license to behave badly two weeks out of the month, and the women claiming the women with extreme mood swings give all women a bad name.

So, to clear a few things up…

20% of women suffer no pre-menstrual symptoms at all

80% of women suffer from some combination of pre-menstrual symptoms

20-40% experience moderate discomfort pre-menstrually

3-8% (possibly up to 10%) of menstruating women suffer from PMDD

This chapter is written for those who have partners with PMDD.

But before we get started, I want to say that whenever I read an article, report, or essay about PMDD, if the author lumps PMS and PMDD together as one, or describes PMDD as a "more extreme version of PMS," I view that entire document with skepticism. Because if they can't get that fundamental fact correct, then to me all information in that document is suspect.

And now, a quick primer on the differences between PMS and PMDD.

PMS deals primarily with physical symptoms. Bloating, aching, cramping, tenderness, fatigue, headaches, food cravings, and mild mood swings are the most well-known of the more than 150 symptoms possible. Some irritability, tension, sadness, weepiness, or any combination thereof is par for the course.

The major component of PMDD is mood swings in the extreme. PMDD affects your brain's capability to regulate itself, and therefore affects just about every other hormone in your body. That's not to say a woman with PMDD can't have bloating, aching, cramping, fatigue, cravings, and other physical symptoms. If she does, it may well be that she suffers from **both** PMDD **and** PMS, and once she gets her PMDD under control, all she'll be left with is some PMS.

Frankly, I think most women with PMDD would be thrilled to simply suffer some form of PMS. Because PMS is to PMDD what a headache is to a migraine. There is a distinct difference, and that difference is *biological*—not mental. The biology of PMS and PMDD share many similarities, but at some point they split into completely different paths. An explanation of that is beyond the scope of this book.

For now, it's enough to know that PMS and PMDD are two completely different things.

That's not to say your relationship won't benefit from the advice presented in this chapter if your partner simply has PMS. But to make things clear: I am not talking about dealing with PMS anywhere in this book. I am talking about dealing with PMDD.

1. **Both you and your partner should make notes on a calendar or use some sort of app to make you aware of when she is most likely to be pre-menstrual.** This can be hard if her cycle is not regular, or she is approaching menopause, but do the best you can to identify patterns. An explanation of my pattern is provided in Flashback #2 (Chapter Four) in this book, A Perfect Storm of PMDD, and can give you an idea of what symptoms to look for.

Period Tracker is one app I have heard recommended several times. WomanLog is another. There are also several period tracking apps available specifically for men, but I would avoid those that treat a woman's cycle as if it's a joke. You know, the ones that tell you when to run for the hills. Running away from a relationship never solved anything.

On the flip side, if your partner is in denial, and claims there's nothing wrong with her—track her cycle separately. In many cases, the man can tell before the woman that she's entering her pre-menstrual phase, because he's watching from the outside, while—either consciously or sub-consciously— she's distracted by trying to cope with (deny, suppress, compensate for) the unwanted changes going on in her brain and body.

Please note: There are women who are in complete denial that anything different is happening to them, and then there are women who know what's happening, but "don't want to deal with this right now" because they are too busy to, and so they pretend nothing is happening, and that they aren't feeling any differently than usual—until it's too late to do anything about it, and the episode erupts full force.

Determine which type of woman you live with, and keep track accordingly.

2. **If she's indicated that this is what she would prefer, try to stay clear of her until the episode passes.** This has nothing to do with you, or her love for you. It's due to her heightened sensitivity to any combination of the five senses. She literally can't handle any more sensory input—be it bright lights, loud noises, touch of any kind, strong smells, or even certain foods. If a woman with PMDD has allergies, they can be exacerbated pre-menstrually. If she has any other condition, such as arthritis, diabetes, lupus, or fibromyalgia, those can be exacerbated as well.

Even if she's otherwise healthy, during episode of PMDD a woman is literally a walking bundle of nerves.

Unfortunately for both of you, this heightened sensitivity and very real discomfort can be so distracting that it makes her unable to focus on things like questions, requests, conversations, or simple instructions. (Now you know why she forgot to put coffee in the coffeemaker when she made coffee.)

Take the first one, for example: You have a question that requires some thought and consideration.

Examples would be:

Major purchases—house, car, appliances, maybe that boat, motorcycle, or sports car you've always wanted (not a good time to bring it up)

Health decisions

Financial decisions

Employment decisions

Decisions involving having or raising children

Vacation plans

Any change of routine or structure in your life

Why? Because during a PMDD episode a woman's brain is not functioning properly. This has nothing to do with how intelligent she is. This is her brain chemistry being disrupted due to the hormonal shifts taking place in her body. During a PMDD episode it can take all of her concentration simply to focus on the basics of getting through each day. If you come at her with anything resembling a major decision, it could overload her brain and cause a meltdown.

So if she asks for space during that time, please give it to her.

3. **Be patient.** Dealing with anybody on a short fuse can be challenging. If she snaps at you, or does something that irritates you, don't lose your temper and fight back. It won't do any

good, and in most cases will only make things worse. Just (discreetly) take a deep breath, maybe say a prayer, and ignore whatever she just did that bothered you. Remember that she's not normally like this and she'll be herself again soon.

4. **Do not enable immature or abusive behavior.** I've said all along, *PMDD is an explanation, not an excuse.* Being emotional does not excuse inappropriate behavior, any more than being drunk excuses offensive behavior. If she's being immature, yelling, shouting, stomping, snapping, cursing, slamming or throwing things, don't respond with your own immature behavior. She at least has an explanation for it—a biological explanation. What's yours?

Stay calm and leave the room if you have to, until she settles down. Let her know you'll be nearby, but you can't have a conversation with her when she's upset like this. Believe me, she knows she's being irrational. But without conscious effort at awareness, she can't stop herself any more than she could stop an allergic reaction. If you calmly say you'll be happy to continue this conversation when she's feeling better, things will settle down a lot more quickly than if you respond with your own emotional outburst. In my original blog post on this same subject I suggested pointing out to her that she's being irrational or immature, but I have since abandoned that idea. Telling people who are behaving irrationally that they are being irrational does not add to the conversation. It only frustrates and angers them more. So walk away. Simply refuse to engage.

5. **As long as she's behaving like an adult, listen to her, even if she's not making any sense.** Try to figure out what the REAL problem is. If she's complaining about something

that's never bothered her before, or doesn't usually bother her, most likely what she's saying is "I feel miserable, and there's nothing I can do about it, so I'm looking for something else to change and hoping that will make me feel better." This is a time of true desperation for her. She's looking for *anything,* rational or irrational, that will make her feel better. This is a good time to suggest she take some time out for herself, maybe a hot bath, or a cup of tea and a good book, or whatever soothes her soul. Let her know you support her need to have a little time to pamper herself in whatever way makes her the happiest.

But beware of sending her out on a shopping spree. Retail therapy will only make things much, much worse when the mood has passed and the bills come in.

6. **Don't take it personally.** During an episode of PMDD, you can count on her emotions getting the best of her, and she'll probably question your relationship. She might question you. Might question her whole life and everything she believes or stands for. This is normal and natural for a woman during an episode of PMDD. As mentioned in Number 5, she's feeling helpless, and sometimes when people feel helpless they look for other things they can control, and that might mean bringing up topics or suggesting changes that trigger *your* emotions. It's like some deep, dark part of her wants to push *your* buttons, set off *your* triggers, make *you* feel as out of control as she does.

I call this the PMDD brain, the brain that takes over when you are in full-fledged PMDD crisis mode, and yes, it can and will bait you if given half a chance. The PMDD brain is reptilian in its desire to destroy any and all obstacles in its path, including her, you, your family, your relationship, and anything near and dear to either one of you. Think *The Terminator*, or any one of those movies rife with robotic killers.

It's not just you the PMDD brain seeks to destroy. It's her, too. From the inside.

That's the part people who don't have PMDD never understand.

Her brain does not care what happens to her in all of this. It has literally taken her body hostage.

Can you even begin to *imagine* what that feels like? Your own brain seeks to destroy you? Studies have shown that approximately one-third of women who suffer from PMDD attempt suicide. Fifteen percent of those women succeed. God only knows how many more contemplate killing themselves every single month, but from the volume of posts on the subject in several public forums, it happens often, and regularly, in some cases like clockwork.

Truly, your best defense against her PMDD brain is to stay level-headed and calmly say, "Okay, I understand." What you understand is that you're still the same person she loved before her PMDD episode kicked in, and her change in perception of you and her life overall is the PMDD talking, not her. It's almost as if you are slowly raising your hands in the air and saying, "I don't want any trouble," to someone who has taken your partner hostage. Just like she needs to separate herself from her PMDD, you need to realize that this destructive behavior is not coming from her, the woman you love, but from an entity inside her, caused by a missing connection in her brain. Fighting her, fighting *it,* by whatever name you want to call her PMDD, can only end badly for both of you.

7. **Be compassionate.** Think about a time when stress or physical changes made you hard to get along with. Have you ever been sleep-deprived? Maybe you had an accident or were in the hospital, and the chronic pain made you want to lash out at everybody. Again, put yourself in her shoes. Not only is she experiencing uncomfortable physical symptoms, but her hormones also ebbing and flowing, making it almost impossible for her to know from one moment to the next how she feels or what she wants. Then her fight or flight reptilian PMDD brain kicks in and all filters are gone.

Think of the effect testosterone has had on you, like when you get sexually aroused, or on any occasion when you felt aggression or rage. You remember how you felt caught up in the emotion, caught up in the moment, how it made you want to say and do things you ordinarily wouldn't say or do?

That's what's happening to her.

Again, her PMDD brain is primed to win at all costs, no matter who or what is destroyed in the process. To *her* brain, this irrational argument about who walked the dog or took out the trash the last time *is* life or death.

That's how skewed PMDD makes our thought processes. We see every crumb of dissent as a full frontal attack on everything we think and believe. PET scans of a woman's brain during PMDD show the same configuration as that of a combat veteran with PTSD.

This is real, folks, with no easy solutions.

8. **Be forgiving and reassuring—but not patronizing.** Her insecurities will definitely come into play during an episode of PMDD, and with her heightened sensitivity, and her PMDD

brain serving as a kidnapper and bully, every negative thought she has will be magnified ten times over. If she doesn't consciously stop the negative thoughts, they will flow through her mind in an endless loop of lies.

Can you imagine your own brain lying to you repeatedly? All day long?

If you can get her to talk about her thoughts, fine. Some women won't want to, because they know the thoughts are irrational, even while they are having them. They just don't know how to stop them. Nobody wants to share irrational thoughts, and then remember the irrational things they said when the episode is over. To a woman with PMDD, when the episode is over, it's OVER. She wants to get on with putting her life back on track. This is usually why, when the episode is over, she acts like nothing happened. This is part of what makes you, her partner, feel crazy.

Remember, PMDD doesn't make sense. It is caused by a brain that is not working properly.

So if she feels unloved and insecure, she'll probably act out, which will make you not want to be around her, which her brain will tell her "confirms" her negative thoughts. Most women feel insecure about their bodies to start with, maybe even their lovemaking, child-rearing, housekeeping, creative or professional skills, and if they're in any way insecure about *your* feelings for them, this is when that insecurity will come out.

So try to give her a few extra compliments (and don't be offended if she doesn't believe you, or snaps at you for it), and— if she'll let you (remember those heightened sensory sensitivities)—be more affectionate. If she won't let you near her, don't make her feel badly by taking it personally. Deep inside, she wants you there, by her side, fighting this bully in her brain with her. But her PMDD brain knows that, and won't allow her to show any vulnerability or weakness to its enemy.

Guilt is the last thing a woman with PMDD needs when she's feeling unlovable. Tell her you understand and you'll be around if she changes her mind.

That could well be all it takes to melt her defenses.

Chapter Twelve

———— ♦ ————

Even More Comments from Readers

We're around halfway through the book now, so I thought you might appreciate an opportunity to learn about the tragedy that is PMDD as it is reflected in relationships overall. There is no doubt in my mind that you will recognize yourself and your situation in the comments that follow. If nothing else, you can take heart in the fact that you are not alone.

More so than the other comment sections, this one contains comments from both men and women. Again, any responses from me are written in italics. There is no requirement to read this chapter. I have included it only to show you there are two sides to this debilitating disorder. On a side note, based on what you have read in this book so far, you may now be able to tell which of the following relationships will succeed—and which ones will not.

———

I have read so many things on PMDD and nothing has ever been more correct than this... I will be showing this to my boyfriend...Thank you.

~\|/~

What this means is you must look to many aspects of your lifestyle to really be rid of PMDD. You must focus on your physical health, your mental and emotional health, your spiritual well-being if you will, and your social health as well! This sounds like quite a lot, but in reality you can make a lot of small changes to your life bit by bit, and start seeing dramatic improvement of your PMDD.

~\|/~

We got engaged after she left me on one occasion and we were set to get married. The accusations continued and basically there was no consistency in the relationship. It was like an emotional rollercoaster. It did not make sense. Anyway, we didn't get married as it became so stressful ... She was literally all over the place, coming and going, moving in and out, it was absolute chaos. I couldn't believe what was happening every month. My work suffered as I couldn't sleep and I lost my job, got another one, and then lost that as well, due to not being able to focus on it.

~\|/~

The advice here is good, but not always easy to keep a level head about. I *think* this is what we're dealing with, but it always becomes the worst about a week AFTER the PMS part...

which means it sneaks up on her quite frequently, and I don't always have the energy or patience to deal with it.

~\⁄~

I'm just worn down with being the target every month.

~\⁄~

The worst part of it is the uncertainty. I know that at some point my wife is going to change and project a thousand negative emotions right into my head, then be as calm and as normal and loving as the girl I fell in love with, but with no acknowledgment of the turmoil that just ripped straight through the heart of our relationship.

~\⁄~

Daily I work professionally negotiating with aggressive, overly emotional and irrational people, but nothing compares to the frustration and hatred that can flare up when I find myself drawn into one of my wife's episodes. Losing track of her cycle is the dumbest thing I can do. I have a calendar with everything PMDD related written in code...Just in case.

~\⁄~

I won't sugar coat it with positive think. It's a hard path to choose, and after a few years of focused learning, tracking her cycle, watching for triggers, evaluating what works and what doesn't, you then have to learn how to control **yourself** as well as your wife's environment every half cycle.

~\⁄~

It's VERY HARD to get any man to do all the above; they simply do not understand. Even when I explain it, he still does things to worsen the condition. He's told me if I keep up with this every month, he will leave me.

~ఌ~

I am only 24 and think I have PMDD to the extreme level. I have suffered ever since i started my period and it has caused me to destroy so much of my life (the bits i love most)!!! now after being in a relationship for 8 years and only just realizing this is what I have it is very comforting to think i can help my partner!!!

~ఌ~

It's easy to say "It's not her fault," or "She can't help it." But being emotionally, verbally and physically abused by a woman with PMDD Is STILL abuse! Do NOT tolerate it! Yes, make a decent effort to suggest help. I would suggest video recording all PMDD episodes. Do so for a few months. Then show her how BAD her behavior is. Do it in a counseling session preferably. DO NOT TOLERATE ABUSE!

~ఌ~

As a person who has captured their PMDD gf on film and showed her the results. I HIGHLY discourage that. An explanation of the behavior while she is calm and rational with no PMDD episode works the best. A video will just ignite depression and anger.

~ఌ~

I am so overwhelmed. I have been married for almost two years and have only recently been informed that the reason for the now apparent monthly crisis we have endured was due to PMDD. We are a day or two into what appears to be this month's cycle and already I am being verbally assassinated and demeaned in it seems every possible way. She will cut me down badly and demand an apology if my reaction isn't loving. Her focus will remain on demanding an apology (even if one is not due) while continuing to be degrading for days.

~✲~

I am trying to understand how she must be feeling. It's difficult when she claims she gets along fine with everyone from work and her family and that it is just me. She has made some progress as she is the one who shared this cause with me. I asked her if this was the week but she denied it. In the beginning she was physically attacking and caused noticeable dental damage. She attempted suicide almost two years ago as well.

~✲~

I am frustrated that I am not doing good at handling her incredible mean statements as I have some hope that if this diagnosis is accurate that she may not mean all these terrible things even though they seem convincing.

~✲~

Yes, the PMDD brain can make terrible things sound very convincing. That's one of its strongest talents.

~✲~

I have had this and far worse for much longer. When PMDD takes over she will try to destroy you with words and deeds. It seems to be evil personified. But when I have looked into my wife's eyes the terrifying - yet somehow reassuring thing - was that this clearly was not the love of my life raging before me but a completely different person. The real woman was - is - the wonderful person that graces my life in between these nightmarish descents into sheer and utter hell.

~⋎~

It has been an ongoing and bruising battle all through the years. The children are a real blessing. They have had a rough time but know that their mother is wonderful when she is not transformed into something frightening by PMDD.

~⋎~

I've been going through this for 3 years now. The only way I can describe it is Ground Hog Day from hell. The way she looks at me, the stabbing words. I've only recently learned of this disorder, I didn't know what was going on every month. I'm happy to have this info, because at least I can see I'm not alone and as hard as it is to believe during an episode, it's not her fault. It's so hard not to take it personal when she is so cold and vicious. I just don't know if I have the strength to go through this hell every month for the rest of my life. But, when the episode ends and she is back I fall in love with her all over again. I'm so lost at what to do.

~⋎~

My wife and i have been married for 12 years, and this started 18 months ago out of nowhere 6 months after our son was born. All these stories are what's happening to us. PMDD has stolen my wife, and our lives. She is deep in denial, but after showing her these and other stories i hope she gets it. We have been in an episode for 15 days now, this is the longest lasting one. Probably because her period is over a week late. It feels like i am fighting for my life, and the pure hatred towards me is harsh. When she gets her period this all goes away and we have a week of normal till it starts again.

※

I've been married for 18 years and I recall hints of PMDD every so often for the first 13 years but the past five years have been a powder keg of anger and violent profanity-laced one-sided arguments. I and my oldest daughter wondered where is this coming from. I took the blame for the outbursts, thinking it was something I said or did, but my daughter said, "Dad, you're not doing anything to cause this." And the more I tried to make sense of the monthly train wreck that is my wife the more nuts and angry I got. Then I noticed there was a pattern or a cycle to these episodes. She became indifferent, angry, irrational, emotional, destructive, and physically abusive. She denies there is a problem and if I persist she snaps so I ease off and tell the kids to steer clear of mom when she seems angry. Divorce has crossed my mind but the saving graces are our beautiful kids. They deserve a mom, a dad, and a home.

※

I have been in and out of a relationship with the same wonderful woman for three years. She has broken up with me anywhere from 7-9 times. It is absolutely predictable. The break ups are inexplicable and all happen right before her period. During or after her period she loves me again and wants to get back together with me...anywhere from two to five days after we break up we are back together.

~·~

I've been reading various PMDD websites for the last 3 years and have heard lots of stories that have helped me. From a man's perspective, this is seriously tough. After about 4 months together (seeing each other twice a week) I started to notice things I didn't understand. I'd get accused of things that I hadn't done, like fancying other women, and I would spend hours defending myself to her. She would regularly say inappropriate things. She'd storm off and regularly misinterpret things I said. I would always beg her to come back and I would apologize to keep the peace.

~·~

It takes everything i have to suppress it at work and it does come out... I've lost two jobs in my life due to PMDD. I've ruined more relationships with bfs and friends though... And yes i notice i come home and unleash it and i feel like a piece of crap after... I will show this article to my bf. He doesn't believe me on any of it and just says i'm crazy and need help... That makes me very angry and when he responds to my outbursts negatively it makes it hard....

~\I/~

I love this girl so much and she is incredible. Beautiful, funny, intelligent. Everything. Unfortunately she has left me for good now it seems because we weren't making any progress and she is now allegedly with someone else. I'm heartbroken but need to focus on getting my life back together. I've contemplated finishing my life over this as I couldn't bear being without her. I've been to counseling myself because I couldn't understand why it wasn't working and it has created some issues with me.

~\I/~

As I have been dealing with the same nightmare for many years, I envy the young men who are not so engulfed in the NEVER ENDING NIGHTMARE. I will not leave my wife, however I am doomed to hell on earth. Mine will not seek help. She is killing us both. Those of us on the target end of this horror surprise epic have limits on what our mind can withstand. Go for a real life, and never look back!

~\I/~

So true! And though I wouldn't leave my wife for anything, I couldn't agree more. If you are with someone and have noted they exhibit this behavior, my advice is to run before you are completely engulfed. Seriously, you are looking at relatively good odds of being miserable for half of the rest of your days.

~\I/~

For me and apparently many other men, it's much too late to turn back now.

I do want to point out that PMDD does end with menopause (when a woman stops having her period), but if left untreated, her PMDD will get a LOT worse before it gets better, especially during the years leading up to menopause, and will leave her prone to Major Depressive Disorder in her post menopausal—or so called "golden" years. Not much to look forward to, which is why I heartily recommend doing everything possible to get a handle on her PMDD before perimenopause sets in.

I have been seeking treatment for years! My issue is, there is none. Antidepressants might help a tiny bit but they also rob you of your "normal time." That is, making you feel very blah when you could actually be feeling like a normal, sane person. My PMDD is so obvious and physical, I can feel it arrive and I can feel it leave. It is sudden and stays for 10 days! It is horrible. People like to think I am making it up or exaggerating. That just makes the problem worse.

My wife is in total denial that she has any problem. I have been away from home for almost two months now. She said she was out of denial two months ago, but then slipped away again. Now she says she doesn't want me back because I made up this illness. We talk on the phone and she says she loves me, and wants to talk to me and everything is good for a few days. Then she starts getting distant, and starts to ignore me. I know her period is due any day now so I'm hoping she pops out of it this time. She missed her period in July and finally got it mid-

August, but we had a huge blowout at that time. Maybe that was the reason for her not asking me to come home that time. When we talk on the phone she cries almost the whole time, she says she wants to be with me, but she is confused.

~\!~

She is confused because her true self wants to be with you, but her reptilian PMDD brain is taking no prisoners. Seriously, you cannot imagine how hard a woman with PMDD must fight her very own brain when it is trying to destroy everything she loves. Sometimes she wins, but most of the time, she does not. And everyone involved suffers for it.

~\!~

I think I have PMDD. I just realized that every month for a couple of days I feel very irritable, I even rage and normally I am a very calm person. I feel like quitting my job and I question every single aspect of my life. Last week I put my relationship at risk because I behaved very badly with my bf. I embarrassed him in front of his friends and on our way home I screamed, I hit him, and I told him he could walk away from me.

~\!~

My girlfriend and I have been dating for 3 years, she is 42 yrs old, and I believe she has SEVERE PMDD. She takes Zoloft and double doses a week before (when she doesn't forget) and can't take BC due to past reactions. Last weekend I went over to her place (one week before her period was due) and stayed the weekend...she worked Sunday but I made dinner and cleaned her house (which was a mess) before she got home. We watched a movie and I would say had a fair evening...She is usually distant and cold during her episodes...She's very affectionate when she is not. The next 2 days she was off from work so on her last day off via text I said I was going to come down and she said, "Well, what if I have plans?" I asked, do you? She said no. Mind you, this is never an issue... I recognized right away I was being baited for a fight... (In the most caring and understanding way possible) I said, "I can come visit on a different day."

But she hung up on me.

~ ⚬ ~

I have been reading blogs for men who deal with this and it helps a lot...we all are dealing with EXACTLY the same women. Everyone seems as stressed as I am...some of the stories are even a little funny...because I identify with the anger and sheer resentment she treats me with during these times. The worst part for me is being ignored, sent to voicemail, sending a text and getting no response, etc. She has a high pressure job that she excels at and I can't help but resent her clients that see and speak to her more than I do during her episodes.

~ ⚬ ~

I love this man profoundly. I want to marry him!!!! He is very disappointed (I can tell). I even had suicidal thoughts. I am going to look for help but I have to do it by myself because he'll believe that I'm trying to give excuses. I take care of my relationships and my job like precious diamonds and then one day I wake up and I want to destroy everything... And the worst is the guilt and shame afterward.

~ ⚬ ~

I have cried my eyes out. She would and will not look into the matter. It has only become worse. Now I am "single" again after 20 years. I miss her ....

~\/~

Brother, if it has gone that long with her in denial, refusing to seek therapy or help, and disregarding what she has done to you, then you are better off this way. I know it may not seem that way at the moment, but stay strong and determined and focus on always moving forward and relearning how to take care of yourself. I'm in the same boat as you, my wonderful (sometimes, and deep down always) wife of 8 years will become my ex-wife this week. As much as I long to show her these sites, with the hopes of happily-ever-after, the one thing I keep coming back to is I can and will sit down and talk about her [PMDD] and textbook BPD *[Bipolar Disorder],* but not until the divorce papers are signed and final. If something miraculous happens subsequent to that, so be it. Otherwise, with absolute certainty, I will be better off and lead a much happier, fulfilling life whether alone or with somebody else. It hurts now and that will continue for a while, nothing you can do about it other than refuse to let it stop you from living your life. It, and you, will get better with time and distance, and the hurt will diminish and come less often. The more you do for yourself emotionally, socially, and spiritually, will hasten the arrival of happiness, and better yet peace and contentment.

~\/~

Keeping you, her, and everyone like us in my prayers.

Chapter Thirteen

———◆———

Tips for Partners Dealing with PMDD

Top 20 Tips for Partners Dealing with PMDD

Unfortunately, my research has uncovered a complete lack of serious information for men on the subject of PMDD, so here it is, short and sweet, a list of the top 20 things you can do for your partner with PMDD.

1. Believe her. When she tells you what she's experiencing, **believe** her. Even if it doesn't make sense. Because PMDD doesn't make sense. The symptoms are as unique and individual as the woman having them.

2. Do not tease her. Do not make fun of her, as this is a serious and often debilitating condition. Would you tease a combat veteran for having PTSD? During an episode, a PET scan of a woman with PMDD's brain shows the *exact same configuration* as that of a vet with PTSD. This woman's brain truly believes she is under attack, and will respond accordingly. (This will cause her to do and say things she would never even consider during her non-PMDD days.)

3. Chart her symptoms daily, either together or on your own. If she refuses to admit there's a problem, then do it on your own so that you can be prepared for when the storm hits.

4. Consult your chart or app when considering social events, activities, or vacations and such. Surprises and big decisions come under this heading, too.

5. Learn as much information as you can about PMDD from reliable resources. If they have a product to sell you, any type of product, proceed with caution.

6. Understand that if it is not treated, her PMDD will only get worse. It could end up as Major Depressive Disorder.

7. Help her to find a doctor who will listen to her and help her. This may take several tries, as most doctors are not trained in the treatment of PMDD. Traditionally trained doctors will only offer you birth control or antidepressants, since they are the only drugs medically approved for treatment of PMDD by the FDA. Your best bet is to find a naturopathic doctor or nurse practitioner.

8. Don't let her negative thoughts and feelings get the better of her—or you. If she shares them with you, gently remind her it's the PMDD talking, not her, and postpone any major changes or discussions/decision making for a few days.

9. Be supportive and encouraging as she tries different things to feel better. Make a note of what works and what doesn't. Share this with her doctor. Do not blame her if any medication she is prescribed does not work. It does not work for most women. Science does not yet understand the brain well enough to know what is biologically going on during an episode of PMDD, despite what the television ads tell you.

10. Help her to get enough rest. Sleep is when our bodies re-regulate themselves. If we don't have enough (sleep) time to do the work needed, we start the day at a disadvantage.

11. Join her for moderate exercise. Exercise is always more fun with a friend. I have found a walk of 45 minutes can buy me up to two hours of PMDD-free time.

12. Encourage her to eat healthy. Avoid alcohol, caffeine, sugar, sugar substitutes, energy drinks, anything made with high fructose corn syrup, and white rice and flour, for starters.

13. Buy her some high quality dark chocolate. Keep it on hand for the bad days.

14. Do what you can to keep stressful situations to a minimum. PMDD feeds on stress.

15. Do not accept any behavior that is abusive. Ever.

16. Do not return such behavior if it happens. Calmly walk away and resume your conversation when she is more in control of herself. Be firm about refusing to engage when she is out of control or abusive. When she gets this way, the PMDD bully in her brain is in full control, and determined to destroy whatever it can.

17. Remember that she literally is not herself during an episode of PMDD. Try not to hold the things she says and does against her. It's not personal, and it's not about you. It's the bully that has taken over her brain egging her on.

18. Be as comforting as she will allow you to. If she won't let you near her, let her know you will be nearby if she needs you. To her brain during this time, allowing comfort equals weakness. Weakness equals vulnerability. Vulnerability is dangerous to the PMDD brain.

19. Don't expect her to be full of sunshine and laughter when she's not having a PMDD episode. A healthy, balanced, and emotionally well-rounded woman feels every emotion—not just the good ones.

20. Last, but not least: Do not blame every time she becomes irritated, annoyed, angry, afraid, or upset on her PMDD. Nothing is more irritating than having a genuine concern or grievance, and being told, "It's your PMDD again, isn't it?"

Maybe it is, and maybe it isn't. Take the time to check her chart to see if she's supposed to be having an episode, and then carefully sort through (usually by talking it out) and separate what is her PMDD and what is a genuine fear or concern on her part. Encourage her to feel and express the full range of emotions, just like people without PMDD do.

More than anything, a woman with PMDD just wants to feel normal. These 20 tips will go a long way toward helping your partner do just that.

~~~

More Tips For Those With Partners Who Have PMDD

The previous section, while it will go a long way toward stabilizing your relationship with a woman in the throes of a PMDD episode, was barely the tip of the iceberg. So here are some more tips and information on how to cope with your partner when she's feeling her worst.

Once again, most articles I've read were about how awful it is for the man, who has to deal with all sorts of aberrant behavior on the part of his partner. There doesn't seem to be much understanding or empathy for the woman actually going through the brain changes over which she has no control.

Her responses to it, yes, she does have some control over those, depending on her level of self-awareness. But for the most part, her reptilian brain has taken over and is simply telling her to survive at all costs—with no thought for collateral damage.

So the first thing I want to re-emphasize is empathy. **Put yourself in her shoes,** and my guess is you'll discover you wouldn't want to have a body and brain you have no control over for several days a month. How would you feel if your thoughts—due to a biological disconnect between your brain and your mouth—came out of your mouth as something else entirely—something actually hurtful to those you love the most? How would you feel if no matter how hard you tried to eat right and/or stay in shape, your body suddenly just puffed up like a water balloon and wouldn't cooperate? What if it actually undermined all your best efforts by bringing on intense cravings for things you know you shouldn't eat, cravings for things that actually make your condition worse?

This isn't about her appetite, it's about her brain, screaming for fuel, for carbs, for glucose, and it doesn't care where or how she gets it. The PMDD brain is like a parasite, only it doesn't care if it kills its host. The PMDD brain does not reason. It cannot reason. And caught up in the middle of its insatiable demands is a woman who *knows* that what is happening is wrong, but does not know how to *stop* it.

How would you feel if for *up to half of each month*, nothing you thought or said or did made sense?

One article I read said women could be touchy—touchy!—about being labeled as a raving lunatic for a few days a month. As if the women involved had no business being so sensitive. It also said very few women will admit they're affected by PMDD. Would you feel comfortable telling people, "Oh, don't mind me, my mind just goes berserk every now and then?" Would you want the strange looks that come with such a statement, would you want people steering a wide path around you because you just admitted there's something not quite right about you? Would you want them declining to hire you or trying to take your children from you?

So don't try to be helpful (or antagonistic) by pointing out her PMDD symptoms. She's well aware of what she is feeling. Anxious, edgy, jittery, depressed, clumsy, fat, foolish, frightened, sleepy, weepy, ravenous, disorganized, out of control...the list goes on.

Even more important is that you don't use any of the above symptoms to goad her into a PMDD rage with sarcasm. We all know men who deal with stress through humor. Even if she loves your sense of humor on her good days, this is not the time to express that aspect of your personality.

Your best bet is to save your meant-to-be-funny comments and war stories for your buddies, and simply act like nothing out of the ordinary is happening at home. Help to make your partner feel as accepted and normal as possible.

This does not mean you have to accept any kind of behavior she throws at you. Abuse is abuse, whether your partner means it or not. Again, PMDD is an explanation, not an excuse, and you should never accept abusive behavior under any conditions.

I also can't say this enough: Don't spring any big surprises on her. Remember she's doing everything she can just to cope with her everyday life, to stay on an even keel in a body that is physically betraying her, and emotionally tilting her from one extreme to another. Her goal is to just get through the day, one step at a time, without being labeled crazy. Big news, big plans, big surprises can wait for a day when she's better equipped to handle them.

But if you forget: Do not trust any big decisions made while she is under the influence of her PMDD. This includes decisions she may come to regarding your relationship. If she says she wants out…do what you can to stay calm, and wait until the storm passes. If when it does she still wants out…then you have a different problem, and she might really mean it.

Take it easy on social activities. If you felt like an acne factory or a beached whale and couldn't seem to control what you put in your mouth (or what popped out of it), would you want to go to a party? A food binge can be great fun, if that's what you want to be doing—if that's your way of celebrating good times or good news. But if you're watching your weight— and what woman isn't at one point or another?—taking her "food binge" show on the road is the last thing she wants to be doing.

The same goes for her emotional outbursts. It's hard enough to keep a lid on things at home. Do you really want to put her in a situation where she spends the evening either snarling at your friends and family or weeping at every misinterpreted comment? Because a PMDD brain will always focus on the negative, and even if you didn't say or mean anything negative at all, even if you compliment her, her brain is being flooded with negative thoughts and images, and eventually the dam will burst— putting a huge damper on your evening out.

And then she'll feel miserable about it. The misery comes from the woman, not from her PMDD brain. The PMDD brain is satisfied when she is miserable, because it has succeeded in its mission—ruining your (and her) day/plans/evening/event. Whether it did or did not, and whether the PMDD-ing woman admits it or not, she will always blame herself for anything that goes wrong during these dark periods of time in her cycle.

Be understanding of her cravings. Just as men do, women seek comfort food when they feel miserable. During a PMDD episode, a woman will especially seek carbs. Doing so is a natural way to boost the level of both glucose and serotonin in her body, and she knows this on a subconscious level. Where it gets confusing is the food and advertisement industries have done their best to convince us certain foods and drinks are healthy when they are not. So while on a very primitive level, your partner's body is craving something to make her feel better, what manifests is a desire to eat everything in sight in the hopes of finding that magic solution. Not to mention the reptilian brain is on the hunt for fuel and doesn't care where it comes from.

In a surprising turn of events, I've discovered it's best to have PROTEIN on hand when these cravings strike. Eating carbs simply creates cravings for more carbs. So I go for the protein now. Eggs, cheese, chicken or fish. I have given up my bedtime snack of whole grain cereal and milk for something containing protein instead, and my symptoms have dropped drastically. But I still eat my dark chocolate when my body tells me it wants chocolate. I can go three weeks without even giving chocolate a passing thought, and then suddenly, it's all I can think about. But it MUST be a good quality dark chocolate. When we consume large amounts of cheap chocolate candy we are looking for the same effect, but in the wrong place. The added calories from the sugar and fat that come along with the added amount of chocolate needed to reach the same mood boost as a good quality piece of dark chocolate only causes our PMDD symptoms to worsen.

They also cause us to gain weight.

But sometimes, the woman's mood dips so low that nothing short of a pizza or plate of lasagna will do. If that's the case, then go for it guilt-free. You might even plan pizza or Italian night around her cycle, and see if that improves things.

Take on some of her workload. Whatever you can do to help out, do it with an attitude of love, not resentment. If she asks you to help around the house, do what she asks. If she wants you to run an errand, please do the same. The slightest bit of effort to appreciate what she's going through will go a long way toward soothing her, and is it really worth the effort to argue over who emptied the dishwasher last?

It's true that things that don't usually bother her will bother her greatly when she's having an episode. Just keep in mind who your real partner is, and go along with what she says. The sooner you do, the sooner her episode will pass. Why is this? I'm no scientist, but I think it has to do with her body releasing bonding hormones.

That's right, bonding hormones, oxytocin in particular. Google it. Stress (and the accompanying stress hormones) will prolong her episode. Oxytocin, (and the accompanying calming hormones), can bring a reprieve to the episode. So if you want the madness to end sooner, the best thing you can do is find a way to get her oxytocin flowing by doing what she asks, as long as it's a reasonable request.

If you're a mature adult, you know what reasonable and unreasonable is. We don't need to go into it here.

Treat her like you appreciate her. Every woman loves to be appreciated, no matter what mood she's in. During an episode of PMDD, with all those negative thoughts running an endless loop inside her head, your partner needs extra special care. Reassurance is always nice, but might not be believed or accepted. Understand that the negative thoughts in her brain are overwhelming the positive ones you're trying to get across. The PMDD bully in her brain is also refusing to allow her to show you any weakness or vulnerability. But you can overcome this.

Be patient. Be persistent. Let her know you care, and you're there for her if she needs you. She'll meet you more than half way if she possibly can.

If she doesn't, it's because she can't yet. She doesn't understand enough about what's happening to her to stop the train of negative thoughts in her mind. It's not because she doesn't want to, or doesn't love you. (Unless she truly enjoys being a drama queen, and that is a different situation/condition/disorder altogether.)

It's not about you at all. Remember that, and don't take the negative things she says to you personally. In a few days time, the woman you love will return, and when she does, it would be a good time to discuss what may have gone wrong between the two of you during her most recent episode.

A lot of women will want to forget what happened, pretend it didn't happen at all, and that's quite normal, but not the best way to deal with it. Talking it out with your partner when she's feeling herself is the best way to prevent unwanted behaviors and situations in the future. For her to pretend it didn't happen is grossly unfair, and the best way to make you, her partner, feel as crazy as she feels. This can only drive you, her partner, into anger or down that slippery slope to depression, which does neither of you any good.

All a woman with PMDD is looking for is the same thing everyone wants—love and acceptance.

The strangest thing is, the more we accept, the less we'll have to. What we resist persists. So don't fight your partner's PMDD. Go with it, roll with it—and watch the storm waves grow smaller over time.

Chapter Fourteen

Readers Speaking Out

Again, there is no obligation to read these, but they may help you to feel less alone. As always, any responses from me are in italics.

Your writing gives both hope and comfort, not to mention the advice is truly good and might save someone from this suffering.

Two thoughts:

1) Men suffer from PMDD too. I am considering seeking treatment for my developing distress/depression. I am not certain, but I think my body has learned to sense my wife's coming PMDD episode. I get depressed/irritable a day or two before PMDD sets in.

2) God bless those of you willing to stay and love your wife with PMDD. The grace of a marital vow is key to this. I do not mean to be callous, but those of you who are saying "my girlfriend" might consider that since you have not yet made a promise "for better or for worse," you should seriously consider that this woman might be better off living a single life and being able to have the quiet, peaceful environment she needs to avoid exacerbating her PMDD each month.

PMDD can spiral downward if not treated. Medical treatment is iffy and getting the peace-and-quiet treatment is almost impossible with children. You, as a father, will one day conceive children. Strongly consider if you want your child to grow up with a mother who drives them through hell for a week or two EVERY month. Breaking up with your girlfriend and suffering that loss now might be the loving thing to do for the sake of the children you will conceive with a different woman, a wife that does not have such a grave, debilitating, and destructive (to others) disorder.

I look back at the warning signs during our courtship and know I could have saved her, my children, and myself much suffering. I thank God, however, for the grace of the Sacrament of Marriage that carries us all through the suffering as we share in the Cross of Christ. I know that, by using that grace, each of us will be able to stay faithful to Love.

―※―

Today I realized I must have PMDD. The past week has been like a trip to hell and back. I am not totally out yet, but seeing the light. My husband-to-be is sleeping, and I am filled with emotional pain and fear....but I

believe that's the PMDD. The extreme negativity was so powerful this month. I am so grateful that I am more than willing to face this, because I KNOW I act mean to him, and to my sweet mom. The two people I love the most, and my inner self-loathing decides to call some shots. I am aghast at this. I am a little overwhelmed, and, like I said, hurting pretty badly. My significant other really needs his rest, and without this [blog] to focus on I might have woken him crying and begging for his attention. This is a really scary thing. But I know I will find ways to help it and to cope. Thank you for being here, and thank you for listening. Good luck to all the fellows out there who try to understand and offer love during a confusing, painful time.

⌇

First off i want to thank you for this site, it's a great thing you are doing here. Until you, all i ever seemed to find on PMS or PMDD was a simple warning of mood swings and irrational behavior, but no particulars to compare to. What to expect, what's not acceptable.

⌇

In putting in all of this energy to insure she is okay, when do the man's feelings come into it? I noticed through reading your tips for men that it doesn't say a lot about how a man is feeling or could feel in this. I'm not sure if I am the only one who gets Sexually Frustrated out there but when your partner never wants to be intimate due to PMDD & never wants to be intimate when not

having an episode either I'm left feeling un-loved, alone, depressed, sad & more. Is this normal? What do I do to help myself in this situation?

～⋎～

I'm afraid I can't address how a man is feeling or could feel in this situation since I am not one and I try not to talk about things I don't know about. My goal here is to help women with PMDD to understand what is happening to them in a way they can hopefully share with their partner. My best guess is your situation goes beyond PMDD and therefore I am unable to address it. Because my information shows that a woman with PMDD craves more affection during an episode, but is also super-sensitive to rejection at that time, so if she is not in a positive, healthy, and supportive relationship with someone who understands what is going on, all kinds of things can go wrong.

Each partner has to do their part when it comes to PMDD. If she is not doing hers, then no matter what you do, how understanding and supportive you are, you can't make the relationship work. A good forum for questions like yours can be found at mdjunction.com. Type in the words "PMDD and men" for a list of appropriate forums. The Experience Project also has several pages devoted to sharing stories about PMDD for both men and women. These are personal account sites, not medical information or treatment option sites. Still, you may find some solace in sharing your story with those who understand what you are going through.

～⋎～

This is such a debilitating, isolating and exhausting condition that I don't even know where to start.

～⋎～

I'm a stubborn man but not without compassion. I'm 46 and my now ex girl friend is 45. We managed to make it for just over a year. At the beginning it was magical; she would be my last and forever love. She did warn me that she would get severe PMS and that [the] full moon would also affect her. The episodes would come with no warning, we would have a wonderful evening together and the next morning she would phone me, a totally different person, then the texts would start. At first i would reply but eventually i would put my phone down and walk away. She would attack me on all fronts, my ability as a boyfriend, my ability as a father, where i live, how i live, she would demean the things i'd do for her, and tell me that most everything i bought for her was worthless and ugly, all the way down to my performance in the bedroom. It always starts with her accusing me of cheating.

‑‑‑

I am almost positive I suffer from PMDD but have become much more aware of the symptoms in the last few months, I think having the coil fitted could be contributing to this. I am in a new relationship and the last thing I want is for this to be affected by my symptoms. I definitely suffer from the insecurity and paranoia as well as all the rest and I don't know how to raise it with my boyfriend as I don't want him to think I'm mad or that this is a massive problem that is not worth dealing with. Outside of my PMDD I am a very rational and secure person.

‑‑‑

After reading the comments above PMDD just seems such a burden to inflict on someone you love, and particularly someone that is a really good person and just doesn't deserve any of this.

~.\l.~

To you husbands and boyfriends...how do we redeem ourselves?? We can't go back and change what we did or said, the guilt stays and the anxiety of knowing that no matter how hard you try, you are going to blow it again... that in itself adds to the stress which in turn worsens our PMDD. How do we reconcile a relationship that we destroy every month??? Is separation the only answer?? Or do we all just suffer on???

~.\l.~

I am desperate to find a way to manage this condition before I do any damage to my relationship. It feels like a ticking time bomb and one that I have had to fight tooth and nail to control so far.

~.\l.~

This, in essence, is the fundamental struggle between the woman with PMDD and her reptilian PMDD brain. The fight is debilitating, exhausting, and seems un-winnable and endless. Many give up trying. Many medicate to achieve numbness. Studies have shown that one third of women who suffer from PMDD attempt suicide. Fifteen percent of us succeed in these attempts. PMDD truly is hell on earth for everyone involved.

~.\l.~

I love this woman more than she will ever know. I wish i could be stronger for her but her words and actions are destroying what self esteem and confidence i have left.

~·~

My other half of 2+ years has PMDD. I have learned to overlook her mood swings and the things she says to me... i know it's not her true real feelings at all. With her i can tell by her tone of voice, and how she types her texts. i guess you can say i read her well. i know it's not good to point out her moods but sometimes it is better to be honest with her. i know throughout this time of the month life can and will be hell. but at the end of the day she is the love of my life and she knows i will walk the fires of hell for her even if they are in our home...

~·~

As a man, I am experiencing some extreme frustration dealing with and understanding the unbelievable mood swings presented to me monthly by my girlfriend. I have no other explanation but PMDD. She is in absolute denial about anything being wrong at all. She wants me to apologize for things I do not do or for things that are routine and normal except for during the PMDD time of the month. She is so intelligent and it is hard for me to understand why she does not realize that something is going on.

~·~

Ok, I am a wife of a wonderful and loving man who has put up with what I now know is PMDD for 10 years. He feels like he has to goad me all the way to a emotional blowup that includes horrible words and accusations and talk of divorce on both our parts, until I "snap back" and realize I have lost it, which I usually do. Afterward I feel guilty, depressed, and full of shame that I said those horrible things and threw things and have actually slapped him! I don't even know where my hand came from, all of a sudden it was slapping him!?! I am "normally" a kind, happy, loving gal. I fear now that the only resort is to separate and spare us both any more agony.

⁓

I'm writing this when I'm well and happy but the days are ticking down to the full moon (oh yes, in one of life's ironies I not only get PMDD but it hits on the bullseye every full moon). I've lost relationships and many friendships to it. I have become so desperate I'm going to my Ob/Gyn to discuss removal of my remaining ovary (my other ovary was removed due to endometriosis). However I have discovered taking away my right ovary could cause many other serious health issues (turns out the hormones don't just send us loopy, they also perform many other tasks around the body, ie: keeping the heart and brain healthy) so it just may not be viable. So I'm back to thinking about regular exercise, changing my diet drastically for the better etc etc. PMDD is like living with an unstable volcano inside...you never quite know when it's gonna blow...

⁓

I have posted on several different websites about my experiences with dating a girl with PMDD. I spent 3 1/2 years of my life trying to calm my then girlfriend down and to try to get her to seek help. She has a history of problems in her life and also mental illness in her family. I believe that ALL of these problems come from PMDD. Her mother had severe problems and her father couldn't cope with the constant roller coaster ride. He had mental breakdowns and developed an alcohol problem to cope with it. My ex has inherited the wild PMDD mood swings for 2 weeks of EVERY month from her mother. I loved her to bits but my life will be better without her in the long run. The only thing you can do is put up with living on an emotional roller coaster or walk away from a PMDD woman. Sorry, but I tried harder than I have tried at anything in my life and it still didn't work. You would not believe the things she'd say to me/problems she caused. If I had married her it would have ended in divorce as she was so out of control and unstable. Maybe yours isn't as bad but I wish you luck. You may need it...

The best advice I can give is to acknowledge how she feels and put her worries to rest when she isn't voicing them. My girlfriend is so thankful to see that I understand her and I feel like we really make progress. Women with PMDD already feel crazy when they are overwhelmed with these symptoms, so it helps them to relax when they know you understand.

The first step is making the choice to figure it out for the both of you. Then figuring her out, and then you have to figure yourself out, and stop yourself from reacting. Once you've managed all that then you need to try and talk to her, help her help herself. This is hard because as far as she knows, it's you that has the problem.

~*~

I am currently having a tough time with these issues, as my girlfriend honestly believes that I provoke her into fights and force her to make amends before the fight will end. I want to accuse her of playing mind games with me because I am often the one to put out the fires after she has a panic attack. It is the hardest thing to be a gentleman and show compassion toward that special woman in your life when she labels you as a horrible person.

~*~

The best treatment that I have found is a non-generic Fluoxetine, Agnus castus, Evening Primrose Oil, B6, D3, Calcium, Zinc, Magnesium, Vitamin C, a healthy diet, very little alcohol, adequate rest, moderate exercise and do not go hungry or starve yourself.

This is what my partner takes and it has returned her back to her normal self. If she misses one part of the above treatment, I know that she will turn into a monster at some point and make my life a living hell.

I hope this information helps someone out there. Female partners in same sex relationships also need advice. I was one of them and I researched the condition and found my girlfriend a really good doctor. Another thing is to be careful when using hormones or the pill to treat PMDD as it can often make it worse.

─❧─

I can vouch for all of these: B6, D3, Calcium, Zinc, Magnesium, Vitamin C, a healthy diet, very little alcohol, adequate rest, moderate exercise, and do not go hungry or starve yourself. I don't take the fluoxetine, have never tried Agnus castus, and I took evening primrose years ago but now I take EFAs, or essential fatty acids.

All of the supplements named above I take DAILY, not just in the second two weeks of my cycle. Just be sure to take the B6 along with a quality B50 complex, as the B6 works best in concert with the other B vitamins. Thank you for sharing your "formula" for success!

You are also absolutely right in that using synthetic hormones or contraceptives to treat PMDD can often make your symptoms worse. Each brand of The Pill has a different level of synthetic progesterone (also known as a progestin) in it, and several studies have shown this progestin component of the formula to be the reason moods worsen while on it. Several studies have also shown the estrogen component of birth control pills to increase your chances of suffering from a blood clot, stroke, and/or breast cancer.

─❧─

My partner takes all of this daily. This week she missed a meal and hasn't been taking some of her vitamins. She has been pure hell this week. I want this to end but I love her. It is just so much work and I can't stand the verbal abuse. I wish she would be responsible and just take the medication and supplements and buy more or tell me when they run out! I am so depressed and

anxious when she gets like this that I have been considering suicide.

~•~

I am now giving up. I can't take her abuse anymore. Our relationship was so great to begin with. Now I am frightened and treading on eggshells in our home. She is a monster. Why won't she just take responsibility for her health and even her life? I am ending our 5 year relationship with a sad but relieved heart.

~•~

I diagnosed myself with PMDD a long time ago. I don't want my spouse to feel like some of you—actually I know how it feels because I, too, had a parent with it. It is absolutely miserable to lose your shit every month, to go from confident & fun to irrational & insecure—no way to live.

Chapter Fifteen

———◆———

When Your Partner Won't Get Help

PMDD Wars: Supportive Partners, Women in Denial

Three years after I started my blog in 2010, I learned of a segment of the PMDD population I'd left unaddressed—mainly because I had no idea it existed. My blog posts with tips for men were written in response to the many posts I was seeing from women with unsupportive partners. What, they wanted to know, could they do to help their partners understand their PMDD?

But since 2013 I have heard from both men and women who love their wives and girlfriends, and would be more than willing to do whatever it took to help her to deal with her PMDD....

Only she's not interested. Because she's not the one with the problem, *he* is, and if he can't deal with that, well, then...

Sound familiar?

It happens in a lot of relationships, and not just those involving PMDD. One partner is trying to work things out, and the other is in denial. Unfortunately, this is a sure-fire recipe for failure. For a relationship to succeed it has to have two consenting adults. Two people behaving like grownups, each taking responsibility for their part in making the relationship work—or not work. It's not about power, control, or changing the other person. It's about doing your part to show your partner that your relationship is a priority in your life, and that you want it to last.

You don't do that by:

Playing the blame game

Expecting your partner to change

Trying to change your partner (for their own good or any other reason)

Running from the problem by working too much or never being home

Ignoring your partner's needs

Being abusive to your partner

Denying there is a problem

Relationships require compromise, day in and day out. They're not about one partner giving up all sense of self to cater to the wants and whims of the other. It's a balancing act, and one that needs adjusting and readjusting daily. It's hard enough to have a successful relationship between two healthy people.

Throw in some PMDD and your troubles increase exponentially.

But they don't have to. Whether you believe it or not, a woman **does** have choices when it comes to her PMDD. She cannot control when it hits, or how severe it may be, but she can, with a *lot* of practice and self-awareness, manage her reaction to it. This is not easy, and takes diligent effort every single month. But she can either take the path of least resistance and give in to her seemingly uncontrollable urges, or she can take a stand and say, "I am not my PMDD. I am better than this."

Her PMDD is not who she is, not the real woman. Root yourself in this knowledge and stand firm. Refuse to let her PMDD brain get the better of you. Refuse to let the negativity win. Sure, she will still be weepy and edgy and anxious and irrational at times. Accept that that happens, but help her to work toward not letting it have free rein during an episode. Everyone slips up now and then, but to totally immerse yourself in negativity and irrationality...that doesn't do anybody any good—especially the children.

A woman with PMDD needs to think of her children if she can't do it for herself. Don't they deserve better than to see their mother not even *trying* to get along with her supposed partner?

This completely boggles my mind. I myself entered a PMDD episode recently. I knew it was coming, I could feel the storm approaching, and all I wanted to do was to be held. Unfortunately, the circumstances for that to happen didn't fall in line. It was payday and my husband was feeling flush. He called and asked if I wanted to go out to dinner at our favorite restaurant.

I reluctantly said sure. I was only going to heat up leftovers anyway. Now I wouldn't have to do even that. In short, I adapted. I decided to let myself be pampered another way since I couldn't have what I really wanted.

But all night long, he kept asking, "Is something wrong? You seem distracted."

Something was wrong, and I *was* distracted, but distraction is also an occupational hazard for a writer, so he's used to it.

Finally I said, "I can feel the storm coming."

He knew what I meant.

He took me home and I went right to bed.

We spent the day apart on Saturday, seeing to individual tasks. I felt all right most of the day, probably because I didn't have to interact with anyone, but around 5:00 p.m. I had an intense craving for carbs.

I had a snack. At the time, my go-to PMDD snack was whole grain cereal with milk. Shortly thereafter my husband arrived and off we went to church...where I could not stay focused to save myself. My mind bounced from thought to thought to thought.

Afterward, out of milk, we went to the grocery store. I had three things I wanted to get: milk, Brazil nuts (for selenium), and cat food. It took every ounce of my concentration to stay on task, to simply remember those three items, and remember where each was located in the store. Since by now I was feeling completely miserable—head pounding, joints aching, brain feeling like it was on fire—my mission was to get in, get my stuff, and get out.

In church, I had let my mind wander, but now, I had to corral all those bouncing thoughts and force my mind to stay on track. So deliberately focused was I that the minute we arrived in the parking lot, I jumped out of the car and made a beeline for the store, completely ignoring my husband. As soon as I entered the store, I saw the rack where I had last found the Brazil nuts.

In that moment, nothing could have come between me and my goal.

But they were out of Brazil nuts. They had almonds, walnuts, pecans, cashews, peanuts...but no Brazil nuts. My husband caught up with me as I stood in front of the nut rack, feeling completely derailed and wanting to weep.

I turned to him and said, "I want to cry, because there are no Brazil nuts here."

I then asked him, "Am I acting strange?"

And he said, "Yes, I noticed something was off in church."

"I thought so," I said. "It's that time again. I'm having an episode."

I then turned away and went in search of the milk, once again leaving him behind. As I was walking, I realized I was being rude. I then recalled other times I had walked off without him and realized that **each and every time** it was during an episode of PMDD.

Suddenly it hit me that I wasn't **trying** to be rude—it was literally taking every ounce of focus and energy I had to stay on task. Otherwise I might look left or right, get distracted and we'd be wandering the store looking at nothing in particular until my husband said, "Come on, let's go."

I would then burst into tears for no apparent reason, he would wonder what the hell happened, and our evening would be ruined.

I stopped and explained this to him and we finished our shopping together.

But the whole time, I was feeling very angsty and edgy and primed to have a fight. As he helped me out of the car when we got home, I said to him, "I could start a fight with you so easily right now."

He looked at me in surprise. "About what?"

"That's just it," I said. "About nothing."

I was overtired and achy and weepy and feeling like a toddler on the verge of a tantrum. No lie. Instead I went to bed. Because I know the difference between me and my PMDD.

And because our relationship matters to me.

It might not have been the most exciting ending to the evening, but at least it wasn't filled with a lot of drama that would leave each of us feeling devastated and alone. My husband understood my need for rest and solitude because I was able to express it in a quiet and (somewhat) rational matter. My husband understands my sudden rudeness and self-absorption is not a reflection of him, but rather of my PMDD.

With a different person, it could have gone completely differently.

If I had behaved differently, it could have gone completely differently.

Because inside of me was someone dying for a fight. It didn't matter what the fight was about. All I wanted to do was goad my husband into sparring with me until I could no longer stand my own irrationality and then burst into the tears I so desperately wanted to weep—and blame him for ruining everything. Maybe even blame him for abandoning me or not loving me when he walked out the door in sheer frustration, for lack of knowing what else to do.

Not because he doesn't love me. But because I wouldn't **let** him love me. Wouldn't let him see my need, my vulnerability, my (what my reptilian PMDD brain would call) weakness, and wouldn't **trust** him to take care of me.

The PMDD brain leaves no room for trust.

And if your partner has even the slightest trust issues to start with, she will find it almost impossible to trust you when she is in the PMDD zone.

The PMDD brain is also paranoid.

That does not make your partner paranoid. Once again, it is the PMDD talking when she gets like that, not the true woman you love and live with. Her brain is sending her lies and she is hyper-sensitive, on the alert for an attack from any and all sources. She is not open to peace.

I'm still having an episode. My head still pounds, my eyes hurt, my joints hurt, my back hurts, my brain burns, and I want to cry. There is no doubt I could be drawn into an argument, any argument, with anyone, at the drop of a hat. It may still happen...because sometimes the strength to hold the negativity at bay just isn't there.

But I do know that if it happens, it will only be for a moment, before I catch myself again, and remind myself that I am not my PMDD, and that my blindsided target doesn't deserve to be abused just because I am having a bad day.

No one does.

~~~

PMDD and Denial

So what did I do two weeks ago when I was hit with my latest double header? (Sometimes the PMDD comes *twice* a month, lucky me, and sometimes not at all, due to my increasing age and anovulatory (no egg released) cycles. If no egg is released, you don't get PMDD.)

So yes, this means that this past month, I experienced two PMDD episodes—right on schedule. The first one was to, um, celebrate ovulation, and the second was for the really Big Show...also known as Waiting for Red.

Anyway, while I was in the PMDD zone, I worked, I wrote, and I slept. (Three hour naps are not unusual when my hormonal system gets so far out of whack.) I focused on survival only. I pared my life down to the bare bones, ate take-out from the organic co-op or heated up all-natural frozen entrees, focused on my work (I work at home, due in part to my PMDD), and wrote my heart out. I took walks when I needed a boost in my feel-good hormones. Took time out for me.

But I didn't do any of that until I finally admitted I was having a problem. And so, it got me to thinking. Why was it I waited so long to admit my PMDD was acting up again? Why was I so deep in denial?

Because I had work to do, a schedule to maintain, a life to live. I didn't have time to give in to some strange, intangible brain disorder that keeps me from getting the things done I want and need to get done.

I wanted to be normal.

I cannot emphasize enough how much women with PMDD want to feel normal. We don't want to admit there's something going on in our brain that isn't right. Something that even the medical professionals can't agree on, much less define. We can find a thousand excuses for why we are so clumsy at times, or so ravenous, or irritable, edgy, disoriented, anxious, or weepy. We deny and deny and deny there is anything wrong with us, or that we are in any way acting strangely, because to admit that we are doing so means we will have to stop and deal with it somehow, and how can you deal with something that defies description?

Sometimes it's a battle you just don't want to fight.

Somehow we've convinced ourselves it's easier to ignore the symptoms we can't explain and plow onward. Because that's what women do. We keep going until we can't go any more. Women with PMDD are especially strong and stubborn in this regard. We go and go and go until we collapse. Or until our behavior becomes so erratic or irrational that someone in our life can't stand it anymore and says, "What's *wrong* with you?"

Even then we deny it. There's nothing wrong with me. If you'd just pick up your clothes, fix the faucet, turn down the TV, do your homework, call me, stop calling me, show up on time, take the trash out, *talk* to your parent/child/boss/sibling, move your car, paint the bedroom, fill out the report, mail the letter, do what I ask, everything would be fine. The problem is you, not me. *You're* what's wrong with me.

And off we head into another relationship disaster, be it with our children, parents, co-workers, siblings, or partners.

The bottom line is there *is* something wrong with us. But it's not something we have any control over, any more than we have control over our genetic predisposition to any number of diseases, eye color, or shoe size. And it's not something we can explain, unless we've done a whole boatload of research—only to find out it's different for every woman, because we each live in different circumstances and environments, and the biological rhythms of our bodies are unique to each of us. No two women are alike. Some have some symptoms, others have others. They come at different times of the month. Before periods, after periods, some even before and/or after ovulation. Sometimes it's two short episodes, sometimes the episode starts with ovulation and stays with the woman all the way through menstruation. It can get as bad as leaving the woman with only ONE good week per month.

Who wants to live like that?

My point is we don't have control over when or how often it happens, or how long it chooses to stay, but we *do* have control over how we respond to our PMDD.

And denial is just not an option. Not if you don't want to leave a landscape littered with big mistakes, bad decisions, and tattered and broken relationships behind you everywhere you go.

For a woman to get a handle on her PMDD, she needs to get a handle on herself. She needs to find a way to spend time on herself, spend some time with herself, getting to know her body and unique hormonal rhythms. She needs peace and quiet to do this. She can't do this in the middle of the latest financial, household, work, school, or family crisis.

She also needs to like herself to do this. She needs to believe she is worth the time and effort.

A common problem among women with PMDD is a lack of self-esteem. Part of it is the PMDD bully talking, part of it is a result of her PMDD and the negative things she's said and done during episodes, and part of it comes from other sources which are beyond the scope of this book.

The bottom line is, as her partner, it is within your ability to help her to see herself for the wonderful woman she is; one worth taking the time to get to know, and one who deserves to feel well.

Sometimes I feel like I live a totally self-indulgent life. I do what I want to do, go where I want to go, see who I want to see, and generally manage my life so that it encounters the least amount of stress and conflict. No drama queen here. I don't have time for drama. It only sets off my PMDD, and God knows I don't want any more experiences with that if I can help it.

So I take care of myself. I eat right, I exercise, and I manage my stress. Even then I still get hit with the occasional strong episode of PMDD.

But just imagine if I didn't do all of that. How out of control my life would be. How joyless, how miserable, how sad and self-destructive.

Ignoring PMDD is like ignoring a train bearing down on you. A wreck is inevitable. Studies have shown that if your partner's PMDD goes untreated, it will only grow worse over time, and she can end up with Major Depressive Disorder. Is this what you want for your partner, for your life?

I know it's not what I want. I also know that ignoring my PMDD, denying it, doesn't make me more normal at all.

It only makes things worse.

There are, however, many things you can do to lessen the severity of your partner's symptoms, and most of those things are mentioned either in this book, in my book *PMDD and Relationships*, or somewhere on my blog, and are also free, or relatively inexpensive.

Which is why you don't hear a lot about them. The only ones you hear about are the ones people are making money off of. But no magic pill is going to cure your partner's PMDD, no matter how much you hope it will. PMDD is not a one-size-fits-all disorder. We've got to stop treating it like it is. Putting women with PMDD on oral contraceptives or antidepressants to suppress (not solve) their hormonal issues is like asking every woman to wear a tent dress. It might cover the body, but it's not a good fit.

It's also a huge form of denial. Denial of our individuality, and denial of our biology.

So, again, the first step is to **stop denying we have a problem**. Over forty years later, I'm still guilty of doing it, even with all that I have learned about the disorder. Is it any wonder those who haven't done the research I have are equally caught up in denial? And what about the women who don't even know PMDD exists? All they do is run around thinking they're crazy, desperate to deny it to themselves and everyone else.

114

You can't possibly think it is normal to wake up one morning feeling fine, then slowly start to lose your fine motor skills, become agitated and confused, weepy, exhausted, irritable, and ravenous all before dinner. The ability to wash away all of that with 45 minutes of aerobic exercise is also not normal. The fact that doing so buys you a couple of hours of PMDD-free time is not normal. The inevitable drop in mood and energy level when it wears off is also not normal.

But it is what it is, and it's all we've got to work with. PMDD doesn't do normal. Accept that and just do what you can to get through it. Support your partner's efforts toward good health and wellness. Weed out the people in your life together that are toxic to her. Encourage her to take time for herself, be good to herself, and most of all, when the episodes come…encourage her, in any way you can, not to deny them. Work together as a couple to find your unique, tailor-made way to keep her relaxed and as calm as possible during her episodes of PMDD.

As I said earlier, what we resist persists, and over the years I have found that when I work *with* my PMDD instead of against it, the episodes subside and lessen in strength over time.

Chapter Sixteen

———◆———

Some Final Comments From Readers

Any responses from me are in italics.

———

My wife and I have been together for 17 years and I've only just discovered your blog. For 17 years I've wondered exactly what has been wrong, and now I finally know, just at the moment when I really honestly don't know if I can continue to take the roller-coaster that PMDD puts you on. It's totally devastating to a stable marriage to have one spouse demonstrate how much she loves you and her life for part of every month, and then demonstrate how much she loathes you (and perhaps even the children) the other part. It's like living with Jekyll & Hyde.

———

My wife is expert at hiding her PMDD from everyone else. Only our children and I understand what happens to her. She holds it in around everyone else, but then at home we bear the brunt of her pent up frustrations, which is just the PMDD talking. But it hurts all of us badly nonetheless.

~••~

Exactly the same for me, but for even longer. My wife refuses to even recognize that there's a problem. In some ways, that is the most destructive part. I can't begin to say how devastating it has been. I am simply exhausted. Jekyll and Hyde doesn't come close. You give so much love and get slaughtered in return.

~••~

About seeking treatment, or refusing to, that's part of the PMDD. When things are going well, we feel normal, and see no need to seek treatment, because everything is fine, thank you, and when we are having a PMDD episode, we're trying so hard to ignore it and simply function, that we're either deep in denial, or too depressed to do anything about it. Then, of course, the PMDD brain takes over and treatment is not an option. Also, many women have tried to seek help and been met with ignorance and/or disbelief because their doctors either don't understand PMDD or don't have the time or inclination to learn more about it. It's easier just to prescribe antidepressants and move on to the next patient.

It's hard to be your own best advocate when you're going through these bewildering cycles of anger, depression, anxiety, and feeling somewhat normal. You never know who you're going to be from day to day. Also, when you make an appointment, you're usually at the point where you can't stand it anymore and desperately want help, but then the appointment is three weeks away and by that time, all your symptoms are gone...until the next time. If you're in the middle of an episode when you have your appointment, it's hard to clearly explain what is happening, because your brain simply isn't working right. You can't get the words out, and instead you end up losing it, breaking down in tears, then go home feeling like more of a failure than when you left for the appointment.

So...It's hard to convince a doctor you have a problem when you seem perfectly fine. On the flip side, many doctors are also likely to misdiagnose you as bipolar, or simply prescribe medication to treat your most obvious symptoms if you show up angry, anxious, depressed, and crying. Some may suggest mental health counseling.

Unfortunately, women with PMDD regularly suffer more for it, and for longer periods than are necessary, when dealing with doctors unfamiliar with PMDD.

～∘～

We did have a three month break earlier this year. But then we got back together. Everything was fantastic! We were talking about living together and how we might plan our wedding. Then she became distant again. When I brought up the idea that she may have PMDD, she said she was fine for the three months we had been apart. She did date someone briefly in that time. Is it possible her PMDD could be less severe and more like PMS symptoms for that three months because she was kind of in escape mode...not dating anyone seriously? When we

did get back together, she told me he was nothing...just a distraction. What are your thoughts?

~\!⁄~

It's possible she was fine for the three months she was away. Put it this way: If she was seeing someone else he was new and a mystery and at that point things are usually pretty rosy and you are looking at things you have in common, things to bring you closer (this is whether it be with a love interest or even just a friend to hang out with), vs. things to move you apart. All this finding common ground increases the level of your bonding hormones and in my experience, oxytocin trumps PMDD every time. Nothing like a good surge of oxytocin (in my case cuddling with my husband) to make the PMDD blues go away.

This is not to say she was cuddling with anyone...simply the fantasy of cuddling with someone (even a movie star) can generate the same biological results in your brain. Talking to a friend and feeling heard or understood can generate the same biological feelings; as can cuddling with a baby or playing with a puppy or kitten. Oxytocin makes no distinction between whether it's a pet or a person, or even just being good to yourself. That's why I encourage women with PMDD to take time out and be good to themselves during an episode of PMDD. Rest, relax, do whatever boosts your oxytocin levels and makes you feel ready to face the world again.

So...If she was in escape mode and determined to believe that all was well in her world, then it is quite possible her brain chemistry reflected that feeling and the PMDD was held at bay during those months. Most couples who are genuinely interested in each other have their first major argument within three months...(if one party is not genuinely interested in having a relationship it can and usually does come much sooner), but at that point a healthy couple decides if they want to split or keep trying…and continues to do so with every major disagreement.

If she truly doesn't see the relationship working out, then there is nothing you can do about it, but quite often that is the PMDD talking. You can't see the positive in anything when you're having an episode of PMDD, and the PMDD brain magnifies the negative at least tenfold.

She would have to cooperate with you to learn to manage her PMDD—and you'd both have to refrain from making major decisions of any sort during PMDD episodes—or your life on this emotional roller coaster will only get worse.

So while I applaud your decision to stand by your PMDD woman, just remember you can't fix something YOU didn't break. Since it affects both of you, it takes both of you to get a handle on her PMDD.

⁓

I'm new to this PMDD thing... but I have read a TON on it. I think you are right... There just may be something else going on here than just her PMDD. Her direct, deep cutting insults and criticisms go above and beyond in my opinion. My suggestion is to get out and get your sanity back. Take care of yourself. Hang out with friends of similar mind set. Do some work on YOU! And READ everything you can about PMDD.

Chapter Seventeen

———◆———

Inside the Mind of a Woman with PMDD

The Other Side of PMDD

My wife has PMDD 2 weeks each month. I can now track it on a calendar. The meanness, sharp tongue, irritability, over-sensitivity to the slightest comment... it's all there each month, like clockwork. I used to make the mistake of reacting to her negativity, which results in a showdown at the OK Corral with talks of divorce, etc., etc. Now, I just keep my mouth shut, offer my help, not reacting to the negativity. It's not easy at all. My only escape is to go to the gym when it seems everything I do is wrong in her eyes. But I bear it each month because I love my wife and I know it's not her. I say she becomes Mr. Hyde once a month for 2 weeks, and I just learn to keep my mouth shut. A big exercise in tolerance and patience. If you love your wife or special someone, tolerance and patience are vital. If you don't have them, you will suffer.

᙭

This man is suffering. My heart goes out to him. My admiration and respect go out to him as well, because he loves his wife and refuses to let her PMDD ruin, end, or dissolve their marriage.

What he says is true. "If you love your wife or special someone, tolerance and patience are vital. If you don't have them, you will suffer."

I suspect he is talking about himself, here, but he could just as easily be talking about both of them.

Much is made over the suffering of the non-PMDD partner in a relationship. But let me say this—as much as you are suffering by being the brunt of her emotions, she is suffering at least twice as much on the inside. She doesn't *want* to be doing what she is doing. She is often as horrified as you are by what comes out of her mouth. Yes, in that moment a part of her malfunctioning brain wants you to suffer as she is suffering, but overall, none of us *wants* to have PMDD, much less *every month*.

Let's do the math. The average age of female puberty is 12; the average age of menopause is 51. Round that off to 40 years of menstruation. Multiply that by 12; that gives you 480 months of periods if you never have children, less if you do. Let's go with 450 periods for now. That gives you 900 weeks of premenstrual issues. Divide that by 52 weeks per year, and you get 17+ years that a woman can spend in the living hell that is PMDD.

Seventeen *years,* people!

So yes, to partners like the man on the previous page, I am grateful beyond measure. One, because you treat your wife with love and respect, and two, because you have allowed me to see where you are coming from, and to respond to what you see from the outside with what is happening to me on the inside.

Notice I didn't say what is happening to *your* loved one with PMDD. That, I cannot know for sure, but by explaining what happens to me, I might be able to open the door to a conversation between the two of you about what happens to her.

I'm going through an episode right now. It started about two days ago. I'd like to say I can pinpoint when the slide began, but I cannot. It seems like a gradual shift, a slow sinking into the darkness—as opposed to coming out of an episode, which I have literally felt in my head when my "non-PMDD brain" snapped back into place. The return to sanity can be instantaneous. The gradual slide into anger, despair, and hopelessness can take what feels like forever.

So while this is what you are seeing on the outside—a moody, irrational, unreasonable, emotional, maybe rude, unfocused, uncaring, detached, disoriented, scattered or otherwise strangely acting woman—I'm going to tell you what's happening on the inside. My head hurts, my bones hurt, my joints and muscles hurt. I didn't want to wake up this morning. I feel like I have been drugged. My mouth is dry and there is a tightness behind my eyes reminiscent of a hangover, but I have not had any alcohol. I feel fat and smelly and ugly.

Yesterday, in the hopes of cheering myself up, I decided to organize the photos from a vacation with friends. In every single photo I was in, I hated how I looked. Normally, my looks do not bother me. I know I am me, and I am loved just the way I am. Yesterday, I was obsessed with my body image. Couldn't find enough flaws to point out to myself.

Okay, so that project didn't turn out. Yesterday, I also went to a funeral. We have no choice when these things happen. You either go or you don't. I felt paying my respects was more important than hiding in my cave. I waited until the last half hour of the viewing, so that if anything went awry, I had a natural exit. Nothing went wrong. The funeral itself was lovely and poignant...one of the most beautiful services I have attended...

But it sparked thoughts of death and dying for the rest of the day. Who's going to go next? How long do I have? How many of us will be here next year? What do I want to do with the time I have left?

This very question nearly devolved into an argument with my husband last night. Normally I am happy to live in the moment and let life unfold as it will. Last night there was an urgency, an almost desperation behind my thoughts and words. We need to do this, and we need to do that, and we need to do it NOW.

I will feel very foolish when that feeling is gone next week. I know this already.

If he had argued with me instead of patiently "listened" to me I would have (at least mentally) declared the relationship hopeless and over. There would have been harsh words and an explosion of tears. I suppose I should be happy that I'm only going to feel foolish. Especially if he takes my dark words to heart...while I've blissfully gone back to my "It's all good" mode.

If you were my husband, wouldn't you be confused?

I spent most of yesterday alone, as my husband was busy elsewhere. (He has learned when it would be a good time to leave me alone and takes advantage of that time to work on his own projects.) Even while my PMDD self was irritated beyond words at supposedly "being abandoned" I was glad he was not here, having to bear the brunt of my irrationality. I knew, as he would have known had he been here, that there was absolutely nothing he could do right yesterday.

So it was best that he was elsewhere. The same went for my son. He walked in the door, aiming for a quick change of clothes, and within two minutes I was not speaking to him. It was best for him, and for me. He left after giving me a big hug and telling me he loves me. As I shut the door behind him my thoughts were, "Yeah, right." The PMDD bully in your brain will have you doing this, denying to others that they love you, because your PMDD brain—at the risk of losing control over you—cannot allow you to soften toward anyone you love.

I adore my son, and we get along great. Anybody who knows us knows he loves me, too. He can get manipulative, like kids do, and I let him, like moms do, but the love is always there.

Not yesterday. Even though it was being freely offered, I wasn't feeling it.

Yesterday I was feeling my most unlovable. Old, dumb, lazy, overwhelmed, uncertain, weepy, morbid, incompetent, uncaring, and unkind. In real life, I am none of those things. Yet if anyone had been around me yesterday...if I had not spent the day alone (except for the funeral)...I would have snapped and snarled all day.

Why?

Because I was feeling extremely vulnerable. I was feeling worthless, useless, and like every decision I'd ever made in my life was wrong.

Hello?

For one, that's not even possible. But there you go.

PMDD doesn't make sense.

So I'm walking around feeling gross physically, mentally, and emotionally, and I'm just...well, I'm miserable inside. Nothing can make me happy, and nobody better try, because if they try they will fail—I'll see to that—and if they don't try, well, I'll have something to say about that, too.

It's no wonder I get letters from women with PMDD who fear they will spend the rest of their lives alone. Who can deal with someone like that? Where nothing you do is right for days, sometimes weeks, on end.

Yesterday I could have gone on a rant like you wouldn't believe about what was wrong in my life.

Funny, I was perfectly happy with my life three days ago. Feeling rather blessed, actually.

This personality change is bewildering enough to watch from the outside. Try to imagine what it feels like from the inside. Try to imagine your brain feeding you lies *all day long.* Lies about yourself, lies about your friends, lies about your partner.

You spend all your energy either fighting off these lies in your head, or letting them wear you down, beat you down. Like I've said, PMDD is a bully. So here you are, being bullied by your own brain. You're feeling your worst, and your weakest—your most vulnerable. You want love, support, encouragement, comfort. Instead, your PMDD bully has come to kick you while you are down, for the PMDD brain shows no mercy.

Someone says something to you. In your PMDD state, your brain twists that something around to the most negative interpretation possible.

What are you going to do...fight or flight?

My PMDD brain has me fighting. That's where my brain goes during an episode. Into primitive, reptilian, survival mode. It's fight or flight, survival of the fittest, baby, and I'm going to see to it that you go down in flames, no matter what the cost to our relationship.

The opposite of fighting is withdrawal. Withdrawal into ourselves—where we let the PMDD bully run rampant inside us—and withdrawal into depression—where we accept what the PMDD bully says, and beat ourselves up even after he or she is long gone.

Try living with a bully inside your brain for two weeks a month and see how long *you* last before you lose it one way or another. Either through anger or tears, or both. So yes, while it is undoubtedly hard on our partners and the friends and family who love us, keep in mind that PMDD is no day at the spa for the woman herself. She is doing the best she can with a temporarily malfunctioning brain. The woman you love is having technical difficulties. Her brain is literally not firing on all cylinders. She doesn't *want* to ruin your party, your weekend, your vacation, relationship, or marriage.

She just wants to feel safe, from demons neither of you can understand nor see.

~~~

The Other Side of PMDD, continued

Since I wrote that last section, and since I was PMDD-ing this week, I paid close attention to what was going on inside my head. Thursday I was overwhelmed and angry. Normally I love to feed people, take care of them, give them a hot meal and some home comforts. But my husband, son, and I had agreed it would be "fend for yourself" night on Thursdays, due to different commitments. I was therefore "supposed" to worry only about myself.

But then they both showed up at dinnertime, hungry and neither one of them cooks. So instead of just worrying about myself, I was suddenly in charge of a meal, and in no mood to graciously pull one together. Instead I became like a drill sergeant...you, go set the table, you...chop those vegetables...you're in charge of the microwave...you, get us something to drink.

Not my usual self at all, but I rose to the occasion and kept a lid on my resentments. Even so, later on in the evening, after we'd come and gone to the Christmas show we were all trying to get to on time, I apologized to my husband for being so...well...bossy.

He didn't mind. He said, "You hardly ever get like that. It's nice to see you're human."

This got me to really thinking about PMDD and what's going on inside our heads when it happens. Are we really screwing up, or is our PMDD brain telling us we're screwing up when we are not, and that's what fuels our insecurities and ignites our fights and relationship issues?

Because you know when you're screwing up. Everyone does, except the truly mentally ill. But those of us who aren't don't need people to tell us when we mess up. Because we know it, inside, when we make a genuine mistake. Pointing our failures out to us only makes things worse. (And I am talking about human beings here, not just women with PMDD.) Men and women alike, we all get hurt and defensive and either go into withdrawal or denial—or come out fighting.

So here's my thought: What if we're not really screwing up? What if our PMDD brain has simply convinced us that we are, and so we act accordingly—by coming out fighting? Science tells us that during an episode of PMDD the fight or flight response kicks in—or, rather, the response kicks in, but then doesn't leave like it's supposed to. Instead, the switch stays on for the entire episode, which, as we all know, can last for weeks. Remember, the brain PET scans of a woman with PMDD are the same as those of a combat veteran with PTSD. During an episode of PMDD, I can say for sure that your loved one definitely feels like she is under fire—from any and all sources.

It's something to consider, the way our PMDD brains deliberately twist our thoughts to create the most negative impact. Because while I thought I was being overly bossy...he just thought I was trying to get everyone fed and out the door in time.

For instance, and this is just one small example of how my brain doesn't work right when I am in the PMDD zone... I walk around the track at my gym. I time myself. On a good, comfortable day, I can do one lap in one minute. Sometimes I can do it in 55 seconds, when I am pushing myself, and sometimes I'm just not feeling up to par and it takes an extra 5 - 10 seconds per lap.

But on an average day, I do one lap in one minute.

When I am PMDD-ing and force myself to go and walk around the track, I feel like I am moving through molasses and every step is a challenge. Imagine my surprise to discover that *according to the second hand of the clock, I am actually moving at my normal pace of one lap per minute.*

PMDD skews a woman's perceptions. Of everything.

Especially moods, though. Fast forward to Saturday afternoon. I am in a rage. I know I am in a rage. Thank goodness I am alone. I think that is part of why I am in a rage. I don't want to be alone. I'm tired of working (I work at home), and I want to take a break, do something fun.

But at the same time I know that if someone shows up, my husband or my son, that's not going to make me happy, either. Meanwhile I stewed. And anything and everything that didn't normally bother me suddenly bothered me, big time.

By the time my husband arrived to go to church, I was angry and I. Just. Didn't. Care.

But I had spent the day "watching" myself, or practicing self-awareness, so I knew I was angry, and I knew there was no reason (aside from my hormones) for me to be angry, and I knew I was being irrational, and I knew I didn't want a fight.

So I asked him...Do you ever feel like you Just. Don't. Care? You don't care whose feelings you hurt, or who you piss off, or what people think? You've just had it, and you're just going to say and do what you want to say and do?

He said yes, he had felt like that.

I said, "Well, that's the way I feel right now. Like I am going to say and do what I want to, and nobody better get in my way."

"I see," he said.

"I'm just warning you," I said. "I'm in that kind of mood. So that if I do or say something totally irrational, you don't sit there wondering, 'What just happened?' "

"Oh. Okay."

And that was the extent of it. There was no incident. We had no argument. We went to church, and then we rented a movie. We had a perfectly pleasant evening.

But I felt better letting him know what was going on inside of me, so that should I snap, he wasn't taken by surprise.

He appreciated knowing I was on the edge. We settled into a quiet evening together.

"So you can control it?" he asked at one point.

Well...yes, and no.

I can control it up to a point. But when the dam bursts, it bursts. And at that point, I can't control it.

My goal is to keep that dam from bursting. To keep from snapping out on those closest to me.

Because it is my goal, I am getting more and more successful at accomplishing it. But I can tell you of a thousand times where I failed.

Try to imagine walking around with a totally irrational "Don't f*ck with me" attitude going on inside your head. Try to imagine this happening several days a month, like clockwork. It switches on, it shuts off. You have no control over when it does either. All you can do is hang on and hope you (and your relationships) survive the ride.

For instance...take a totally normal exchange at the deli counter when you're in one of these moods.

The deli clerk asks what I would like. I smile and tell her. The clerk asks "sliced or shaved?" This question totally pisses me off inside. I'm here every f*cking week (not true) ordering the same damn thing (close, but also not true) so why can't they f*cking remember (unreasonable expectation) what I like?

Are you seeing how a PMDD mind works?

Meanwhile, I am still smiling and politely answering, "sliced" like I do every time, and feeling like I want to punch the next person who crosses my path.

It's really not about you. (Although it can be, so don't think you're completely off the hook). It's about doing battle with thoughts that come flying out of nowhere and are sometimes voiced before you can stop them. It's about hearing or seeing or doing something and placing the most negative context on it that you can possibly imagine. It's about not knowing what you want or how to make it better.

As I told my husband, "Don't even try to make me feel better right now because you literally can't. You will not be able to win, no matter what you do."

But there are things we can do to keep it from getting worse. Here are some I prefer. Sitting quietly together, watching a movie or maybe listening to music, or taking a nap, or reading a book. Hugging without talking. Going for a walk. Just being together in silence, or at least a peaceful atmosphere.

Together with your partner, figure out what she enjoys or can tolerate.

For me, silence is best, so that I can concentrate on doing battle with the misperceptions raging inside my head. So that I don't suffer information overload and say something I will regret. In short, when I am PMDD-ing, don't confuse me by asking questions, or by wanting something from me. I am using every ounce of control I have to appear sane. This is a time you either need to give to me (your love and understanding) or get the hell out of my way.

There's really no in-between.

Chapter Eighteen

---◆---

It's My Party and I'll Cry If I Want To

PMDD Flashback #3

It's My Party and I'll Cry If I Want To

I got my first inklings something was up on Sunday morning, when I woke up groggy, head hurting, and ravenous. Determined to beat the PMDD blues, I ate a bowl of whole grain cereal (quick acting carbs) and went back to sleep for another sleep cycle, about an hour and a half. The next time I woke up I felt better, more on an even keel thanks to the carbs and the extra sleep cycle, so I vowed to not let my PMDD ruin "my" day.

And it didn't. Not that day or the next. It was my birthday and almost nothing could get me down, although at the oddest times, I found myself looking off into the distance and just wanting to cry.

That was Sunday. Tuesday I embarked on a project that would challenge anyone's ability to concentrate. For hours I sifted through airline websites and travel reservation matrixes, trying to find the best dates, flight times, and price for two seats to Europe—a gift from my husband. The print function on my computer wouldn't cooperate, so I had to hold all the information in my head from screen to screen to screen. My desk was littered with sticky notes on which I'd scribbled the names of potential destinations, airlines, and prices.

So...flights finally chosen, I'm now filling out the information. Here's something new. I need to input the names of who will be traveling exactly as they appear on the identification we will be using—in this case our passports. I call my husband. He doesn't know what his passport says. He says he will check and call me back in less than an hour.

He gets busy and forgets.

My day takes a nosedive. By the time I see him that evening, I'm not speaking to him.

It's that simple.

I busted my brain on the computer for several hours trying to organize a trip *he* suggested. *He* forgets to make a f*cking 30 second phone call. I am furious. Just that fast. And there is nothing he can do to make it right. And I mean no-thing. I am in the mood for a fight. And I don't care who I fight with. My son makes an equally available target. He disappears into his room as I start sniping at both of them, sharp tones and snide comments left and right. I know I am doing it, and *I don't care*. I feel unloved, unappreciated, unheard, unhappy, unhealthy, unfit, un-everything. You name it. No one understands me. No one cares. No one appreciates the things I do around here.

"I see the weekend is over," my husband says quietly.

We had an amazing weekend. Truly amazing. Went to church, went for a sunset walk, went to a festival, met all sorts of interesting people, played miniature golf, went for a drive in the country, cooked a couple of fantastic dinners, slow danced...he even presented me with a 30 minute DVD of a slide show of my trip to Alaska, set to soothing music. It was my birthday and it was beautiful.

But all of that was gone in my PMDD mind. All that mattered to me right then and there was he didn't call me back; he didn't appreciate my time, my work, or me.

His quiet words were my cue that I had crossed the line.

I apologized. Sincerely. Because I knew I was wrong. In the end, though, I went to bed and again, just wanted to cry.

The next morning I didn't want to wake up. All morning I couldn't concentrate, couldn't stay focused on any one task. Couldn't even contemplate writing anything. By afternoon, my brain literally hurt, like it was inflamed or something, and I found myself reaching for my PMDD comfort foods...cheese, chocolate, and oranges.

By evening I knew why.

My period had arrived.

Chapter Nineteen

———•———

The Queen of Denial

PMDD Flashback #4

The Queen of Denial

She's baaaack! I'm talking about my PMDD self. After several months of relatively mild episodes, suddenly I'm hit with a humdinger. I am one of the unfortunate many who have atypical PMDD, (as I mentioned in my PMDD Flashback #2 - A Perfect Storm of PMDD), in that it occurs both before and after I menstruate. Kind of like a hurricane, with my period in the middle, serving as the eye of the storm, where I might feel lousy physically, but I'm clear-headed and things are relatively calm.

So, about ten days ago, I could feel a storm blowing in. I notice I'm starting to get agitated about things that don't usually faze me. I realize I am emotionally looking for a fight, anywhere I can find it. I check the calendar, confirm it's about that time of the month, and warn those closest to me it may be a rocky few days. I back away from conversations and situations I know will set me off, and postpone any important decisions or discussions.

The storm came and went, no major incidents, other than a couple of afternoon naps due to extreme sleepiness. My menses came, and life was good again, aside from the physical discomforts of having a period.

Usually, the second half of my PMDD begins on Day 3 of my period. So when Day 3 came and went with no trouble, I thought I was in the clear, home free, another PMDD episode averted. Kudos to me once again for not letting my PMDD brain get the better of me and wreaking all sorts of havoc in my life and personal relationships.

But this was not my usual period. This one lasted six days instead of three. Not a problem. I'm okay. Life is still good.

But then yesterday morning, I started noticing things. Like I tried to address an envelope, and my handwriting was all jumpy and spiky, like that of a much older person. My hand couldn't control the pen the way it usually does. My typing was off, too. I kept hitting the wrong keys.

No matter. I'm just in a hurry. (Denial #1)

Then I went to a funeral at a church I had never been to before. I got lost. Suddenly I'm feeling anxious, edgy, confused, my thoughts all scattered.

No biggie, it can happen to anyone. (Denial #2)

At the funeral, all I wanted to do was weep.

Not a problem. People are supposed to be sad at funerals. (Denial #3)

I came home and fixed myself something to eat. I work at home, so I started to work in my sun-drenched living room. Suddenly I couldn't keep my eyes open any longer.

Nothing unusual there. The room was warm and I had just eaten. Never mind that the room is equally warm and sunny most days, and I eat lunch every day about the same time and don't get sleepy. (Denial #4)

Finally I give in and take a nap, unable to concentrate or stay awake. It still hasn't dawned on me, what is happening, because Day 3 came and went and I escaped the PMDD bully's wrath this time around.

I wake up, totally ravenous, and wanting nothing but CHOCOLATE.

I still haven't caught on. Or if I have, I'm heading into serious denial: *I don't have time for this nonsense. It's Day 6 and my PMDD is supposed to be over, dammit! I have work to do.*

A friend calls. We agree to meet up later on, go to our movement and stretching class together. I want to know how soon "later on" is. Is it 4:30, 5:30, 6:30? If it's sooner rather than later, I'll wait to eat with my friend. If it's later, I'll eat now. No big deal either way. I just want to know, so I can plan my evening meal accordingly.

Somehow that simple conversation goes totally awry, and I end up in tears.

Bingo. My evil twin has struck again. Now I know what's going on. My PMDD self has returned for round two. My head hurts, my eyes hurt, all I want to do is cry and go back to sleep.

But I'm too agitated and upset to go back to sleep, and I'm so hungry I want to scream. But I just ate a full meal a couple of hours ago. There's no logical reason for me to feel so hungry.

My friend calls back to see if I'm all right. How do I explain that everything is fine....but it's not? How do I explain the contradictions of PMDD? This isn't the type of conversation you want to have over the phone. It's best that the other person can see the glassiness in your eyes, the exhaustion on your face, the lack of energy and slump of your body.

I fix something to eat (healthy carbs!) and work on a small project that only needs minimal concentration for an hour or so. My friend arrives, and I try to explain what happened. She asks, "What can I do to help?"

The only answer I can come up with is, "Just be nice to me. I'm fragile today. Oh, and you might need to run interference for me at class. I'm not feeling very social right now."

We go to class, and all goes well. I manage to muddle through the social aspects of class. (During an episode of PMDD, women with PMDD have trouble coping socially—another reason, aside from the sheer physical pain of PMDD, that your partner prefers to cancel out on social activities during that time of the month.)

But the exercises get the blood circulating, produce the necessary boost in feel-good hormones. By the end of class, which was the absolute last thing I had wanted to go to—at the time I would much rather have crawled back into bed and tried to sleep away my exhaustion—I was feeling 100% again, and had bought myself a couple of PMDD-free hours.

Because in my PMDD-induced confusion and misery, I had **forgotten** what I could do to help myself. Light aerobic exercise. When I'm in the throes of a PMDD episode, and the last thing I want to do is get up and move, *that's the very thing I need to do.* A simple walk is all it takes. After about 30 minutes, I start to feel better. By 45, I'm back on an even keel. An hour of any kind of light cardio activity and all symptoms are gone…

For about two hours.

So by the time I got home, I was back to being myself again. A totally different person. I was able to make it through the rest of the evening without incident.

But as soon as I opened my eyes the next morning, I felt that heavy wet blanket of depression closing in on me again. The iron band around my head, the irritated eyes, like I've been crying (but I haven't), the mental fuzziness, the sense of exhaustion even before I get out of bed.

There's no denying it this time. It's going to be another PMDD day.

Chapter Twenty

———◆———

Why PMDD?

Time for a little more background information on PMDD.

When does PMDD happen? And How does PMDD progress?

You don't get it before your first period. Girls, on average, are now getting their first period at age 12 or sooner. A woman's probability of developing PMDD increases with each hormonal event in her life thereafter: pregnancy, miscarriage, abortion, or birth. (Women do not experience PMDD when we are pregnant, because we are not ovulating.) With each new pregnancy, whether carried to full term or not, our chances of developing PMDD increase. And unless our PMDD is addressed it will continue to worsen with each hormonal event, becoming increasingly difficult through perimenopause, until it stops when we reach menopause.

But don't start cheering yet…if your partner's PMDD is not addressed before menopause, she runs the serious risk of developing Major Depressive Disorder after menopause. The average age of menopause is 51.

So, as I said in Chapter Seventeen, on average, women have approximately 40 years during which we can experience PMDD. Approximately half of those years will be spent in the PMDD zone, less any time spent pregnant, which opens us up to more than seventeen years of time served in PMDD hell.

Seventeen years is a long time to feel and/or be out of control. Seventeen years is also a long time to be on medication, especially medication that studies now show doesn't work more than half the time.

Despite what those ads on television and in your doctor's offices tell you, nobody knows for sure what causes PMDD. All scientists know is it is a biological event that manifests as emotional symptoms. What does that mean? It means PMDD is caused by something that happens in a woman's body and shows/expresses itself in our moods. The closest science has come to defining what happens is that whatever happens, happens in concert with a woman's menstrual cycle, and involves our hormones. The hormones they have looked at the most are estrogen, progesterone, and now a metabolite of progesterone, called allopregnanolone.

Some schools of thought are convinced it has something to do with the levels of these hormones in a woman's body, and whether they are in the right balance or not. But you can't detect PMDD with a blood test, and every estrogen/progesterone blood test I have taken has shown my levels to be perfectly normal, *even when I was in the middle of a PMDD episode.*

I think the best science has come up with so far is that yes, PMDD does have to do with our hormonal fluctuations, but it's more that something goes awry in our brain when processing these normal and natural hormonal fluctuations in our body.

That's right. Something goes wrong in your partner's *brain.*

Not her uterus.

How? ***We don't know.*** All we know is there is a biological "something" in our neuro-endocrine system that happens where our brain does not properly process the fluctuating levels of our reproductive hormones during the second half, or luteal phase, of our menstrual cycle. This leads to a disconnect in the brain, like when a Shop-Vac cord gets yanked out of a wall outlet, or when your cell phone coverage drops. The result of this disconnect "may" affect the level of serotonin in the brain— serotonin being *just one* of several neuro-transmitters that *in part* govern our moods, and our ability to be happy.

This, however, is a theory—it has never been proven.

Ever.

But the antidepressant manufacturers would have us believe this "serotonin imbalance" theory is fact, and this is the cause of our PMDD, because it then allows them to sell us up to seventeen years or more of the "cure." Then, since our PMDD has not been properly addressed from within, and we have long since passed the stage where we became dependent on these drugs, the drug companies can sell us these same drugs to get us through the rest of our natural life.

144

I once bought into these "hormonal imbalance" and "serotonin imbalance" theories as well. Just like any other woman with PMDD, I was desperate to find an answer to the cause of my PMDD that made sense—and these two theories do make sense.

But that is assuming they are true.

And they are not. Having read as much as I have on the subject in the past ten years, I am no longer convinced serotonin levels are the sole culprit for PMDD, if they are a culprit at all. In his book, *Prozac Backlash*, published fifteen years ago, under the heading *Test Tube Studies of Blenderized Rat Brains*, author Dr. Joseph Glenmullen states, "One cannot measure serotonin levels in the brain of any patient. Nor can one measure serotonin at specific synapses. Synapses are the spark plugs between nerve cells, junctions where they exchange chemical messages, and where drugs are said to work."

He then goes on to say that blood levels of serotonin drawn from the arm of a patient are of little relation to what is going on in our central nervous system, or our brain.

So to get around these scientific roadblocks, researchers worked with test tubes containing fragments of smashed rat brains to discover the effect various drugs might have on the human brain.

Keep in mind also that most studies use male rats, because female rats, *due to their swings in hormone levels,* are considered a potential source of unreliable findings.

But back to Dr. Glenmullen in *Prozac Backlash*, who says, "To talk about "selectivity" [as in the case of selective serotonin re-uptake inhibitors, or SSRIs] in regard to smashed brains in test tubes where fragments of dead cells no longer influence one another is irrelevant; to talk about it in regard to living humans is simply folly."

Once I understood how the SSRI antidepressants Prozac, Paxil, Zoloft, and Luvox were tested for treating depression, and where this hypothesis of a "serotonin imbalance" came from—I began to have my doubts. My doubts were confirmed when I read about the more than sketchy FDA approval process for these same drugs, Prozac in particular. Prozac is the first line treatment recommended for women with PMDD by the American Medical Association. You might have heard the words Sarafem, or fluoxetine, which is the generic version of Prozac. All are the same drug. Look them up at drugs.com. Investigate your options. Be aware of the potential consequences. Don't just give drugs to your partner and hope for a miracle. Know what you are getting into.

That's not to say serotonin levels have nothing to do with our moods...otherwise why would we crave carbohydrates? Carbs do increase the level of serotonin in our bodies, and therefore "do" improve our moods. The science of it aside, somehow we already know this on an instinctive level. Whenever a person is feeling down—not just women with PMDD—we tend to reach for our favorite comfort foods— which more often than not happen to be loaded with carbohydrates.

Whether the carbs affect more than the serotonin levels in our brains is for someone other than me to determine. So while I agree that serotonin is involved, it's not the whole picture. But antidepressant manufacturers claim it is, so they can sell us products that in some cases barely squeaked through FDA approval—and have since been shown in clinical practice to be a widely ineffective course of treatment.

More on this later. I now want to say a few things about nutrition. Both of these subjects are addressed in much more detail in my booklets *PMDD and Antidepressants*, and *PMDD and Nutrition*, but today I want to touch on our almost universal ability to, when stressed, reach for the WRONG kind of carbs.

You know what I'm talking about...the cookies, cakes, donuts, ice cream, chips, crackers, pasta, and more. All our favorite foods. For while these carb-loaded delights might temporarily do a half-baked job of lifting our mood, the boost is short-lived. Instead what we get is an exhausting rollercoaster ride of mood swings and blood sugar highs and lows throughout the day—because we would have to eat a boatload of these cheap fake food products to sustain any kind of real mental or energy boost.

Never mind that eating all this junk food only makes us sicker (think diabetes, heart disease, cancer) and fatter—which in the end does not improve our mood at all.

The bottom line is craving carbs is natural. But not just any carbs will do. Simple, refined carbs (like the ones I named above) are out. What we need are the complex carbohydrates provided by fresh, preferably organic whole foods. Fruits, vegetables, whole grains, etc.

But that is not what we reach for. And since we cannot logically eat enough junk food to keep our brains swirling in serotonin, doctors prescribe antidepressants to mask the symptoms of our PMDD.

Again, I'm not at all convinced antidepressants, oral contraceptives (and now the long-acting reversible contraceptives, aka LARCs, the industry is pushing) are medically necessary to treat PMDD. Not as long as there are safer, more natural-to-your-body ways to accomplish the same.

Think about this: Why would anyone want to take a mind-altering medication *daily* for something that only happens a few days a month? I realize some women's PMDD episodes are longer, but for those that run longer than 7-10 days, I honestly believe there is something more than PMDD going on—most likely an ongoing condition or disorder that has not yet been identified—which grows worse as our periods approach. This, as I mentioned in the Introduction section of this book, is known as *pre-menstrual exacerbation,* or PME, of an underlying condition, and there are countless conditions that qualify.

Which is the *real* reason a woman needs to see a doctor for PMDD. Not to diagnose the PMDD, but to rule out whatever else may be making the bulk of her days a living hell. PMDD, in and of itself, is not supposed to last more than one week per month. If it does, there may well be something else going on in your partner's body and she needs to get it checked out.

What she doesn't need is to mask the symptoms with antidepressants and/or contraceptives. Again, what we resist persists, and what we put off dealing with will only come back harder and stronger in the end. We will all have to deal with the consequences of our choices one day, and the tragedy of it is most of us will never connect the two; the worsened symptoms we are having and the drugs we have used to mask them.

Also, antidepressants and birth control come with a host of side effects that can, and in many cases do, make your PMDD symptoms worse. But people rarely consider that the drug may be the cause of this increase in symptoms. We blame ourselves for not responding to the drug, because somehow our PMDD brain has convinced us we are the only one who isn't responding properly while everybody else is doing fine.

This is also not true. All you have to do is Google the antidepressant or form of birth control prescribed to treat your PMDD along with "side effects" and all sorts of posts will pop up. Scientific *and* anecdotal.

So do your research. Don't blindly believe the advertisements. Find out what your loved one is putting into her body. Pay attention to how it affects her. And remember the body never lies. The body *will* fight back. Just like your partner's PMDD brain, her body is designed to survive, and will do everything it can to warn her when it feels under attack—until her body simply wears out from being ignored and cannot sustain itself any more.

Most of us don't fall prey to old age, we fall prey to side effects. Each time a new drug is added to our regimen, our body has a whole new set of side effects to cope with. Doctors routinely prescribe new drugs to deal with the side effects of the previous drugs they prescribed. One example is this: Prozac is a central nervous system stimulant. When it was approved by the FDA, it was approved to be used *in conjunction with a sedative*, like Xanax, to lessen the stimulating side effects of the Prozac. (Think anxiety, agitation, insomnia.)

However, this only compounds the problem and obscures any hope of getting to the root cause of your partner's PMDD. It also leaves your partner at risk for addiction to these sedatives. Not to mention the side effects *they* cause. Grogginess, fogginess, balance issues, memory lapses, missed words, increased risk for dementia, and so many others.

So think about that, and know there are still a lot of safe, easy, *cheap* things you can do to help your partner manage her PMDD. Most do, however, require time and effort. It takes time to make good, healthy meals. It takes time to listen to your body and become aware of what makes you feel better and what makes you feel worse. It takes time to find the right treatment for her particular symptoms. It takes time to sort out what is her PMDD and what is something else, maybe a thyroid problem, or polycystic ovaries for example.

It takes time to take time out for rest and relaxation, and to deal with those messy stresses eating up our hours and days and lives. It takes time to get comfortable with our emotions, to accept and even welcome both the good and painful emotions.

It takes time to work on our relationships.

It takes time to quit using whatever crutches we've been using to get through our ten, twenty, thirty or more years of PMDD.

Think of how many more years or potential periods your partner still has on her PMDD horizon, and how her PMDD will only get worse if she doesn't do something about it.

The average age of menopause is 51.

How old is your loved one?

Can you really afford not to help her?

Do you really want her to spend her golden years depressed or medicated?

You didn't ask for the hand of cards you were dealt. The best you can do is learn how to play them.

The information is out there. Help her to find it.

Chapter Twenty-One

———◆———

I Can't Leave it Alone...

Because I care. Anyone the least bit concerned about the side effects of the drugs being prescribed for PMDD needs to read *Are Your Prescriptions Killing You?* by pharmacist consultant Armon B. Neel Jr., and Bill Hogan. Another book I highly recommend is the one mentioned in Chapter Twenty, *Prozac Backlash*, by Dr. Joseph Glenmullen. Then, you can either take my word for it, or read, *Talking Back to Prozac: What Doctors Aren't Telling You About Prozac and the Newer Antidepressants,* by Peter R. Breggen, M.D. and Ginger Ross Breggin.

For what is Sarafem but Prozac in pink, and what is fluoxetine but generic Prozac?

Did you know antidepressants do not work *at all* for at least 40% of those with PMDD who take them? Thanks to several meta-analyses of antidepressant studies even this 40% ineffectiveness number has been touted as too low. Other studies are finding that antidepressants don't even work better than a placebo for *depression*—yes, the very thing the SSRIs mentioned in my previous chapter were tested for, using rat brains. So how can these drugs truly work for PMDD, whose hallmark symptom is depression?

These questions are addressed in my book, *PMDD and Antidepressants*. This book is about helping your partner to find the right treatment for her PMDD. I only bring up antidepressant failure rates here so that when your partner goes in desperation to the doctor for help, and comes home with a prescription for either an antidepressant or birth control or both—there's a better than 50/50 chance it won't work for her...

And your personal hell will only get worse.

So don't blame your partner for "not trying" if this turns out to be the case in your situation. And if your partner has already tried every antidepressant and/or medical method of birth control under the sun, and it still hasn't helped her PMDD, I want you to know *the fault does not lie with her.*

The fault lies with those who persist in treating us as if we are all the same. The fault lies with those who perform their research on male subjects, and then apply the results to women as well. The fault lies with those who approve drugs intended to treat millions for *years* based on short term clinical studies lasting only a few weeks. The fault lies with those who have a product that maybe eases one or a few PMDD symptoms but advertise that product as an overall cure for PMDD.

They're selling us dreams. The scientific hypothesis they use to sell us these dreams—and these drugs—has never been proven, and *no one* knows what causes PMDD in the first place.

No one.

No matter what they claim.

Okay, so why treat PMDD with birth control? The Pill and several long-acting reversible contraceptives (LARCs) keep you from ovulating, which pretty much everyone agrees by now is the main precipitator of this mysterious shift in hormones that our brains do not process correctly.

But again, using a contraceptive to treat PMDD treats only *some* of the symptoms and not the underlying cause. And birth control medications have their own array of dangerous side effects—including death.

I, for one, am not interested in taking something that could permanently disable (heart attack, stroke, blood clots, liver tumors, vision problems, depression) or kill me when there are so many less drastic options to try.

Tell me, is increasing your partner's chances of suicidal ideation *really* the answer to her monthly suicidal thoughts? When up to one-third of women with PMDD attempt suicide and 15% succeed?

Both antidepressants and hormonal contraceptives can help shift your brain into negative territory within days. It can happen so fast you never see it coming. Antidepressant use in America alone is up 400% over the past twenty years. Since the year

2000, overall suicide rates in the USA have increased by over 20%. (In the fourteen years prior to that, they had dropped over 20%.)

Think about that one for a while.

That so many doctors would so blindly, perhaps even blithely agree to treat suicidal women with drugs that could increase their chances of success at killing themselves makes no sense to me. Especially when nobody really knows what causes PMDD.

The medical industry is playing Russian roulette with our lives.

So watch your partner carefully, each time she starts taking a new medication for her PMDD.

Do we know what contributes to PMDD yet? The answer is yes, but is also as varied as our symptoms. Contributory factors include weight, lifestyle habits, (such as smoking, drinking, stimulant and drug use), caffeine and sugar consumption, stress, trauma, physical, mental, and sexual abuse, and yes, genetics. PMDD can be inherited.

In that case, your partner really "can't" help what happens to her when she's in the PMDD zone. Because it's in her genes. And if it is in her genes, she's not going to be able to cure it with any pills or LARCs.

That's just plain common sense.

I've said it all along: The best any woman can hope to do is *manage* her PMDD. And for that she needs a body that is as drug-free as possible.

So what *can* you do about your partner's PMDD? You can help her to address the things that apply to her situation, and your situation together. I'm not going to touch weight, for obvious reasons. I'm also not going to talk about smoking, drinking, caffeine, sugar, or sugar substitutes. Those are all personal choices, and must be made by the woman herself. If she asks for your help in giving up any of these, all the better, but the desire and determination to quit must come from within the woman herself.

But here are some other ideas:

Exercise – If she leans toward sedentary, encourage her to get more exercise. Two to three 30-minute walks a week will do wonders for her PMDD—45 minutes is even better. Offer to go with her if you would like to, or give her the time to go alone if that is what she prefers. If she's into extreme exercise, she needs to cut back, as moderation is the key for PMDD.

Rest – she needs to get as much as she can, especially during an episode.

Nutrition – there's a reason fresh, whole foods are good for us. They're packed with the nutrients our body, *especially our brain,* needs to function properly. Taking high quality pharmaceutical grade supplements (not the cheap ones from a discount store!) does help, but doesn't by a long shot make up for what we can do to make ourselves feel better by eating foods as close to their natural state as possible.

Foods especially helpful for PMDD are those rich in:

Calcium

Magnesium

Potassium

B Vitamins

Vitamin D

Tryptophan
and serotonin-boosting foods, a list of which can be found
in the Faith and Hope section of my website, under the
Nutrition and Wellness heading, or in my book, *PMDD and
Nutrition*.

Chapter Twenty-Two

———•———

Stress and Women with PMDD

Stress and the PMDD Woman

So what actually *causes* stress in a woman with PMDD?

Well, trauma, for one. Trauma, (such as a life-threatening accident, war, imprisonment, witnessing or being the victim of a violent crime (rape, murder, domestic violence), abuse of any sort, a death or major upheaval in the family, especially one over which you feel you have no control)—any of these can predispose a woman toward PMDD.

How? Incidents of trauma create neural pathways in the brain that can lead a woman with PMDD to *over-react both physiologically and emotionally to normal everyday stressors* in her life by producing an excess of, among other things, her fight or flight hormones. Once this neural pathway has been opened, via trauma, the ruts are established and only get deeper with each new stressor, be it big or small.

To top it off, stress can contribute to further missed connections in the brain.

Other sources of stress include:

Addiction

Women with PMDD are more prone to addictive behaviors, including sexual addiction, relationship addiction, drug addiction, nicotine addiction, alcohol abuse, emotional eating and other eating disorders (like binge-eating and bulimia), all of which bring stress into her life.

Substance Abuse

This has to do with the reward/pleasure center of the brain, which by now we all understand does not work right during an episode of PMDD. What she thinks will bring pleasure or relief from her weepiness and edginess and anger in fact does not, because her brain is not processing information correctly to start with.

As I said in Chapter Seventeen, PMDD skews a woman's perceptions. Of everything. This includes what she sees, what she hears, what she feels, what she thinks, and what she reaches for to numb her pain. Depressed people in general like to self-medicate and jumpstart the reward/pleasure center of the brain with external substances, both legal and illegal. But the PMDD brain *does not respond properly to these stimulants,* leaving women with PMDD vulnerable to addiction.

Adolescent Abuse

More will be explained in my booklet, *PMDD and Abuse*, but for here, briefly, studies have shown that women who have been abused in adolescence are more likely to develop PMDD.

Childhood Abuse

A scientific link has been found between women who were abused as children, and women who develop PMDD. Again, this has to do with the faulty neural pathways developed in times of trauma, affecting the fight or flight response in the brain.

Physical Abuse

Physical abuse has the same effect on the brain as trauma. Women in abusive situations are also more prone to anxiety and depressive disorders, which add to the burden on the brain.

Sexual Abuse

Studies have shown sexual abuse to be a precursor to both Major Depressive Disorder and PMDD, no doubt through the connection to trauma. A link has been established between sexual abuse, PTSD, elevated thyroid ratios, and PMDD.

This does not mean every woman with PMDD has been abused in some way, or is an addict or substance abuser. Nor does it mean every woman who has experienced some form of trauma or abuse will develop PMDD. It simply means that the types of abuse listed above have been scientifically documented as one of several possible contributing factors to PMDD, along with genetics, lack of rest and self-care, and/or poor exercise and eating habits.

Chapter Twenty-Three

———◆———

Things your Partner Can Do for Herself

In Chapter Thirteen I covered 20 tips for partners who live with women who have PMDD. While it would be ideal if all partners did all of these things, that's still only 50% of the equation. The woman with PMDD has to bring something to the party too. Your partner doing all the giving and you doing all the taking does not work *at all*. Nor does it work the other way around.

Even if you've got the most amazing, supportive partner in the world, there are still things you can do to make your PMDD episodes run more smoothly.

1. **Chart your symptoms daily.** Use a notebook, calendar, or app. It doesn't have to be elaborate. Just write a few words each day: anxious, crabby, sad, sleepy, achy, bloated, weepy, craving for _____, snapped at _____. Create your own

list of symptoms common for you. Use your chart/app to get in touch with your feelings and your body. Eventually you'll discover patterns of symptoms.

2. **Consult your chart/calendar/app when considering social events, activities, creative or household projects, vacations and such.** Making major decisions comes under this heading, too. Don't set yourself up for failure by taking on something big when you know you won't be feeling up to it. Don't just try to slog through your life the best that you can…be pro-active! And make sure your partner knows what is going on so he or she can help you with extra support.

3. **Learn to recognize when you are symptomatic, and consciously postpone thinking about anything that needs serious thought until you are feeling better.** If you don't, your decisions will be colored by your PMDD, and you may well end up asking yourself, "What the hell was I thinking when I decided to do this?"

4. **If you only take meds during the second half of your cycle and they take a few days to kick in, consider taking them a few days early** so that they have already kicked in on the first day of ovulation. Discuss this with your doctor if you have any questions. In truth, this second half of your cycle is the only time you should need to take any medication, and in regard to antidepressants, this is how they were originally meant to be prescribed for PMDD—luteal phase only. If you're having trouble with side effects, check with your doctor to see if intermittent dosage is for you.

5. **If you are highly irritable during your PMDD episodes schedule time to be alone.** Don't feel badly or

guilty for needing this and do whatever you can to carve out time for yourself.

6. **If you are prone to depression during this time, schedule time to be around supportive friends**. No sense in going through this alone. Calling a friend or family member over to simply talk in your sweats or PJs helps quite a bit. So does having a good online friend or two.

7. **Shop ahead. Stock the fridge with healthy foods** like leafy greens, fruits, and healthy carbs to boost your energy during this phase. You'll crave junk food and if you already have healthy food on hand you'll be less likely to head for greasy, salty, sugary, and fatty foods that will only make you feel worse.

8. **Understand that if it is not treated, your PMDD will only get worse.** You could end up with Major Depressive Disorder and who wants that when you know it can be avoided?

9. **Find a doctor who will listen to you.** If the doctor won't listen, change doctors. It's your life at stake here. No one has as much to gain from finding the right treatment for you as you do. So take an active part in your own health and wellness. Don't just do what the doctor says because "The doctor knows best." The doctor knows what the doctor knows, and if the doctor doesn't know anything about PMDD, you need to find one who does.

10. **Try whatever you need to try to feel better.** If you don't feel better, try something else. This goes for both medical and natural treatments. If medication works for you, go for it. If it doesn't, don't keep hanging in there, thinking it will get better over time. Your doctor is not you, living in your mind and body. Your doctor can't feel what you feel or experience what

you experience. Only you can know what works for you and what doesn't. With your doctor's help, stop taking anything that makes your PMDD symptoms worse. Trust your intuition and inner wisdom on this. If you don't feel like you have any inner wisdom, then work on your PMDD awareness and cultivate some. My book, *PMDD and Relationships* describes this process in detail if you need additional guidance.

11. **Do not let anyone make you feel inadequate because something that works for others is not working for you.** There is nothing wrong with you if this treatment or that treatment doesn't work. All it means is you haven't found the right solution for *you* yet. PMDD is not a one-size-fits-all disorder.

12. **Move your body.** Fit exercise in—whatever you can, whenever you can. Find a few kinds of exercise you enjoy and mix it up so it doesn't get boring fast. A class here, a walk there, maybe tai chi today and Zumba tomorrow. Just put on some music and dance around the house with the kids or by yourself for a song or two. See if that doesn't boost your mood. Park your car a few spaces away from the door instead of in the closest spot. Thirty minutes of some sort of mild aerobic activity a day is best, even if it's just cleaning the bathroom or carting laundry up and down the stairs. If you have to start with five or ten minute increments, then start there. Anything is better than nothing.

13. **It is essential that you get enough rest.** Sleep is when your body re-sets itself and if you don't get enough of the right kind of sleep, your body doesn't have the time it needs to complete its repair job from whatever abuses you subjected it to during the day (aka substance abuse, smoking, stress,

overexertion, poor diet). The more sleep you lose, the harder it is for your body to catch up, and you fall further and further behind each day. This in part explains why you are so exhausted.

14. **Eat healthy.** Choose whole foods, as close to their natural state as possible. Avoid alcohol, caffeine, sugar, sugar substitutes, anything made with high fructose corn syrup, white rice, and white flour, for starters. Start being aware of what you eat and drink, and as you pour that cup of coffee, know you are contributing to your PMDD, and know that you are choosing to do so. Ask yourself is this candy bar, energy drink, glass of wine, piece of cake worth feeling miserable two weeks from now?

15. **Get some high quality dark chocolate for when the cravings come.** Not that mass-produced stuff that comes in a bag. No matter how good it tastes, it's not going to help you like true dark chocolate will. A bonus is you'll need less of the high quality stuff to feel better, so you might even lose some weight.

16. **Feed your mind and/or funny bone.** Have some meditation CDs on hand, stacked and ready in advance to listen to, or some funny movies waiting by the DVD player to choose from if comedy is your favorite form of relaxation/release during an episode. You can often get/download these from your local library for close to nothing. The same goes for soothing music or whatever your preference is in listening/viewing material. Or create a PMDD basket of favorites tucked into a cabinet for when the need arises. Maybe create a PMDD playlist on your phone or other listening device. Close your eyes and listen when you have a few spare minutes, or are waiting in line, or riding in private or public transportation.

17. **If you snap out at someone, stop, apologize, and explain to them that it's not them, it's your PMDD.** Don't let hurt feelings fester, on either side of the relationship. If they are a stranger, an acquaintance, or not open to an explanation of PMDD, just say, "I'm sorry, I'm having a bad day," and leave it at that. Everybody has bad days now and then.

18. **If somebody is trying to bait you, walk away.** Don't let their bad mood or behavior spark yours. Tell them you'll be back or will continue this conversation when you're both in a better mood.

19. **Ask for help when you need it.** If you don't have anyone in your life who is willing or capable of doing this, find new friends who will be supportive and encouraging. Even if they're just online. PMDD forums and discussion groups abound. You don't need to go through any of this alone. Go to Facebook and type PMDD in the search box if you don't know where to start. Google PMDD groups. The National Association for PMDD is also available for resources.

20. **Do not let your negative thoughts and feelings get the better of you.** Every day, all day long, our minds run rampant with thoughts. Good ones, bad ones, even strange ones. One way to get a handle on this is to learn how to still your mind. But that takes dedicated time and effort. If you're not at a place in your life where you can take the time out to meditate or practice some form of deep breathing exercises, try simply taking three to five slow, deep breaths when you feel anxious, fearful, frustrated, or irritated. You will be amazed at how this helps to calm you. At the very least, when the negative thoughts come, push them right back out of your mind and refuse to dwell on

them. Say to yourself, "That's my PMDD talking, not me," and consciously change the subject.

Remember, (as long as PMDD is your only problem), you are in control of your mind...your mind is not in control of you (even though it very much feels like it, and even though your PMDD brain is doing its best to hijack your thoughts). You need to refuse to give those negative thoughts any air time. If you don't, they will loop endlessly through your mind, creating deeper and deeper ruts, until negative thoughts are all you know. This is in part how women with PMDD become suicidal.

If you find yourself in any way in danger of committing suicide, whether it is due to your thoughts, the actions of another, or due to a new medication you are trying, call the National Suicide Prevention Lifeline at 1-800-273-TALK (8255) immediately.

Chapter Twenty-Four

―――◆―――

Taking Care of You

I thought this book was finished. I sent it to a friend to proof read, and she, a former social worker, came back with the insight that, "The book is all about her."

Well, yes, I said. It's a handbook for partners, giving them ideas on how to help the woman they love in her time of need. It's supposed to be all about her.

No, she says. You have nothing in your book about self-care for the partner—the caretaker. What to do to relieve stress because this is such a stressful situation. They're both suffering stress from her PMDD, and you never talk about the stress the partner feels.

Oh.

She was right.

After a few days of thought, I realized I didn't write about self-care for the partner because one, outside of being a mom, I've never been a caretaker, and two, I've never been a man. I had no clue what men partners in this unique situation could do to relieve stress. Women partners tend to have a more innate sense of the nurturing required for PMDD. In no way do I mean to minimize your stress; in fact, everything I say next applies equally to women partners. But for just a moment I'll focus on the masculine approach, because I do know that trying to relieve stress using the usual go-to choices for men tends to backfire badly during an episode of PMDD. I'm hoping I can shed some light on why.

Sex? You may be taking your life in your hands. Especially if she just wants to be alone, or her senses are so heightened as to be painful (sight, hearing, taste, touch, and smell). Self-sex is usually your best bet there.

Laughing, teasing, joking around? Forget about it. She loses her sense of humor during an episode and will take any and all comments personally. The result will be either rage or tears or both and will leave both of you wondering what the hell just happened.

Drinking? Not good for a woman with PMDD, not good at all. Just because many women with PMDD self-medicate using alcohol, does not mean it's a good idea or good for their PMDD. The same could be true for partners, especially during an episode. Drinking often magnifies any unresolved emotions lurking just beneath the surface. Arguments erupt that neither of you is prepared to discuss. Shouting matches ensue over matters small and large, often ruining any chance of having a calm conversation about the issue at a later date.

Computer games? Internet surfing? One, she's going to be pissed that you're not helping around the house, and two, she most likely will feel neglected if the internet or video game you're playing seems more interesting than her.

Going out with friends? Not a good idea when your partner is in the PMDD zone, as she will most likely feel betrayed and abandoned. This eliminates the usual stress relievers of hunting, fishing, golfing, any kind of sport with your buddies, basically anything that gives you pleasure that does not include her. That's not to say you can't pursue these activities during one of her good weeks—in fact, you should. But more on this in a minute.

I never thought of the PMDD partner as a caretaker before. But isn't that what we are asking you to do? Temporarily take the reins or carry our load when or because we can't? We don't necessarily want you to take care of us (although some women do), but rather step in and take care of what we are unable to take care of at that time—and this includes our children. We want you to have our back; we want you to be our safety net. We want to be able to hand off the ball until we can get back in the game.

PMDD caretaking, however, isn't like other caretaking, in that partners do get a built-in break from the stress of an episode when she is experiencing her good weeks. I don't mean to make light of the chaos you endure during her PMDD days, and it may well take all of her good days to recover your own equilibrium, but it's not like the 24/7 caretaking of a parent or child with chronic health issues.

Still, stress is stress, and a partner's health can be just as negatively affected by a woman's PMDD episode and the guilt and remorse that often follow. So yes, you, too, need to protect your health from the fallout of your own PMDD stress, fallout which can include heart disease, high blood pressure, migraines, depression, back pain, diabetes, cancer, and a weakened immune system.

The first principle of self-care, however, is that it's not so much *what* you do, as the fact that you must see this break/activity as necessary for your good health, and not something to feel guilty about. Ever. Time away from caregiving (or, in this case, away from your partner when she is feeling well) must be seen as an accepted part of a balanced life, both for you alone and for you as a couple. But during an episode, as unpleasant as it may be, unless she specifically tells you to go away and *means* it, it's best that you stay in the vicinity, or at least close enough to check in on her periodically. Especially if there are children in the house.

Honestly, the best thing you can do is take the children somewhere to keep the noise and neediness level at home down. Give mom some space. But if there are no young children involved, then quiet hobbies that keep you in the garage or basement workshop (or tinkering with something somewhere nearby) work best for stress-relief *during* a woman's episode of PMDD. Think woodworking, model-building, gardening, or even reading/writing/painting. Knitting/crocheting is good, as is any kind of quiet, creative outlet. I stress quiet, because so many women are extra-sensitive to sound and light during their days of PMDD. The last thing she wants to be hearing is power tools and the sounds of construction. (So don't think this is a good time to work on that remodeling project she's been after you to finish.) I hesitate to suggest cooking or baking for the same reason; the noise factor. Not to mention the mess that needs to be cleaned up afterward. A woman in the PMDD zone feels overwhelmed. If you like to cook but don't like to clean up, that will only add to her workload and feelings of inadequacy.

If you don't have any hobbies on the quiet side, here are some stress-relieving tips in general.

1. Breathe. Sometimes taking three to five slow, deep breaths can help you to relax and stay calm. Sometimes just one discreet breath is all you have time for, but believe me, it works wonders.

2. As always, exercise is a winner. Great for letting off steam and easing frustration. Anything from pushups to going for a run to hitting a heavy bag, to cycling, yoga, or tai chi works for easing stress. I've suggested that going for a 30-45 minute walk can ease your partner's symptoms when she is in an acute phase of PMDD. If she will let you, why not join her for that walk? Agree in advance whether you want to talk or not talk on these walks. Sometimes a walk in silence with a friend can have amazing results, no matter what the issue is.

3. Step away from the junk food. Actually, processed food makes all of us crabby, whether we have PMDD or not. Once the initial consumption high wears off, we all feel out of sorts; but most of us never make the connection. So stick to good proteins, fruits and vegetables, and complex carbohydrates as

172

much as you possibly can. She needs to eat healthy during this time in her cycle, and so do you.

4. Get adequate rest. Easy to say, so very hard to do. Especially when you have a combative woman on your hands, wanting to have it out right here and now. Among other things, a woman with PMDD will resent your ability to fall asleep when she is so wound up with the negativity in her brain.

5. Look for the positive in all things. No matter what is happening, internally find something good to think about, and do not let her disorder bring you down. Depression in the partner of a woman with PMDD is common—your seeming inability to do anything right or help her can foster this. But keep your happiness pretty much to yourself during an episode, lest she pounces on it in a fit of jealousy.

6. Seek counseling. PMDD does not make sense. Period. Just knowing that means you will eventually need to find someone to talk to. A trained professional would be best; someone who can help you—not add to the problem. Friends and/or relatives may take your side. Friends and/or relatives may demonize your partner. I'm not saying to keep her PMDD a secret and not talk about it with outsiders, but how you deal with her PMDD should be between you and your partner and no one else. A trained professional can help you find healthy ways to communicate your fears, needs, and frustrations. Find one that charges fees on a sliding scale if you do not have insurance. Seeking help is a sign of strength, not weakness. Nobody expects you to have all the answers. Seeking help also ensures that what is private to you remains private. You avoid the added stress of having a friend or relative let something

you've said in a moment of anger or frustration slip. Counseling can be especially helpful when your partner remains in denial about her PMDD.

7. Know you are not alone. When you feel like you are, visit my blog or search for other PMDD blogs and various support groups online. On my blog you will find the latest information I have discovered about PMDD, and can read stories of others who deal with PMDD monthly, stories written by both women with PMDD, and their partners. MD Junction has a forum for men coping with a partner's PMDD. The National Association for PMDD (USA) and National Association for Premenstrual Syndrome (UK) also have many links to resources for information about PMDD.

8. Remember that abuse is never acceptable, and neither is violence. If either you or your partner cannot cope with her PMDD without resorting to abuse or violence—seek help. It doesn't have to be that way.

9. Last, but not least, since her PMDD symptoms can come on so fast and without warning, here are over thirty tips to help de-stress on the spot, or on short notice, most of which are scientifically proven to help lower stress.

Again, take a deep breath. Then take another. Take as many as time allows.

Remember it's not about you.

Find a repetitive motion task to do. (Examples include doing dishes, folding clothes, sanding wood, washing the car.)

Seek the positive in each situation and learn to re-frame.

Find somewhere private to meditate or just close your eyes and contemplate for a few minutes.

Plan a vacation in your mind; something to look forward to when the episode is over. Something to pull you through.

Pray.

Look to nature for inspiration, either in photos or in front of you.

Even a ten minute walk will help.

Or drive home on a route that has more trees than buildings.

Buy some plants to care for, either at home or at work.

Spend time with your pets.

If you don't have any pets, watch puppies or kittens or funny or heartwarming video clips. Science has shown they boost your levels of feel-good hormones.

Read fiction. It takes you out of your world and into another.

Drink herbal tea. Try it. You never know. There are so many flavors to choose from these days.

Drink a glass of orange juice. Seriously.

Same goes for a glass of water.

Snack on Brazil nuts. Or almonds.

Eat a snack mindfully. Something healthy that comes in slices, or bunches, or handfuls.

Grill salmon for dinner, or order it for lunch. Boost your— and her—omega 3's.

Hold hands with someone. Parent, child, friend, partner. It doesn't matter whether you are giving the comfort or receiving it—you both benefit from it.

Write in a journal, compose a song.

Create something. A story, a painting, a poem or sculpture.

Restore something. Take on a refinishing project.

Adult coloring books are very popular these days.

Go swimming. That post-swim pee will clear your body of toxins.

Punch a pillow if you don't have a punching bag.

Put on some music just for you.

Combine the two. Get some plastic or wooden spoons and line up a few pillows on a counter or tabletop or your bed, and pretend you're a drummer. Using earphones, of course.

Find a place to just shake it out; arms, legs, head, shoulders.

Walk away when all else fails. Don't go far, but walk away.

Electronics are rarely a good go-to stress reliever when PMDD is involved, so the goal is to unplug and find peace another way. Too many women with PMDD find seeing their partner engrossed in a television show, video game, or social media a trigger for their rage. To the PMDD brain, it means you don't care about them or their needs. It means your attention is elsewhere, and not on them, or on your relationship (or your family). It doesn't matter whether this is true or not, this is what the woman's brain is telling her, and in that moment, those thoughts are real to her. You are ignoring her, you are no longer interested in her, you find her any number of unappealing things (fat, ugly, lazy, stupid, etc), you would rather be somewhere else, with someone (anyone!) else, and you don't appreciate anything about her.

I've inadvertently turned this section back into being about your partner. But that is what it has to be when it comes to PMDD. You need to know how to deal with her, the woman you love, when her brain is temporarily not working right. The bottom line is you need to treat her gently, and with kindness and compassion. A little compassion goes a long, long way to a woman suffering from PMDD. At the same time, however, you need to be just as compassionate and caring with yourself, because she counts on you to pick up the ball when she drops it, and you can't be there for her if you don't see to your own emotional and physical health needs as well.

So treat yourself as kindly as you would the love of your life, and you'll be further ahead of the curve than most.

In closing, I wish you and your partner every success in finding the right combination of answers that will work best for you as a couple. PMDD is no picnic, and your partner is very lucky to have someone like you in her life, someone who is taking the time and making the effort to understand the rollercoaster ride of emotions that both of you experience every month.

One Last Reader Comment

I found this blog [while] searching for something to help my husband know what to do with me. I feel better now, but I fear I'll regress and we'll struggle again as a family. I have PMDD. I say DO NOT bring it up when she is at her worst. She is completely irrational and doesn't want to answer stupid questions or talk about how she is feeling. [In that moment] it seems so obvious to her that you should know how she is doing. Don't bring it up on a date or otherwise special time between you two. It is better to ruin a good day or week to get her help, than to keep living like how you are and end up divorced.

First, you need to get your wife medical help. When you have an opportunity to talk—not in public—ask her if she's ever had PMS. She may not have realized her moods are associated with her cycle. You're either going to get a "Yes, dumb★★★" answer or a "No, not really, I don't think so."

Depending on how that goes, tell her you've done some research, you think her moods might be associated to her cycle, or, if she knows she has PMS, that it might be something more serious. Tell her about PMDD. Read her the symptoms. Ask her if this is how she feels sometimes. Feel bad for her, say you're sorry she has to endure that every month. Let her know there is help available.

I know it sounds insane. I know you shouldn't have to put up with it. I also know how well I'm doing now and wonder how much better last year could have been for my marriage if my husband would have reacted to me differently. If he could have said, "How are you doing? Not well? Let's get you to the doctor," instead of "You're so mean and I don't have to put up with this." I think I would have felt better. I was already on an antidepressant. It wasn't working.

What I need to feel better is a new prescription and a husband who will back off when I'm irritable and take care of the kids. When I have a bad day, I need him to think, "She's mad, hmm, let's look at the calendar, yep, she's pre-menstrual, I'm going to leave her alone, not mention PMS, and take care of the kids until she feels better."

It might be a few hours, it might be a few days, but it won't be a few weeks like it was last year when he was mad at me for having a bad day; then I felt worse, then there was a fear he'd leave me. I get it, I wanted to leave me, too, but women with PMDD, I'll speak for myself at least, need to feel wanted and loved and worth it to help.

So that is my advice, stranger. Ruin a good day to get her the medical help she needs. Say, "I took next Thursday off work, would you like me to take you to the doctor?" If you have kids, arrange babysitting. It's so hard for moms to find an hour to go to the doctor, especially if she doesn't feel she's worth helping. Even if it's not PMDD she has, make sure she gets bloodwork done. They should be testing her thyroid to make sure there aren't issues there.

Either way, good luck, and from the wife's perspective, thank you husbands who stick it out and deal with us. Some of these marriages seem beyond repair, but husbands can do so much to help. Think of how she is doing and what you can do to help, even if that means just leaving her alone for a bit. She's not rejecting you. She feels like s★★★. Unless she comes to you, your touch will be repulsive. It's not personal, it's just how she feels. Know that she cannot help how she feels when she is premenstrual. For me, I feel angry, tired, sad, and irritable so I am distant to try to protect the ones I love most (from me).

Perhaps your wife [doesn't] care so much if she is mean, but I care. I bet deep down she cares too because she loved you enough to marry you and doesn't want to be mean to you. You don't have to understand it, you won't ever. You just have to love her through it. Hopefully she's worth it to you.

Resources Section

National Association for PMDD (USA)

National Association for Premenstrual Syndrome (UK)

My Blog: Living on a Prayer, Living with PMDD

My Website: Living with PMDD

My other publications, most of which are due out in 2016 — Check my blog or Living With PMDD website **Resources** Page for availability:

PMDD and Abuse
PMDD and Antidepressants
PMDD and Contraceptives
PMDD and Nutrition
PMDD and Relationships

Medscape Overview of PMDD — The best medical overview of PMDD I have found to date.

MDJunction Forum for Men Dealing with PMDD

National Domestic Violence Crisis Hotline
1-800-799-SAFE (7233)

American Foundation for Suicide Prevention

National Suicide Prevention Hotline
1-800-273-TALK (8255)

Printed in Great Britain
by Amazon

85136635R00121